WALES THROUGH THE AGES

Frontispiece: Designed by David Jones, C.B.E.

WALES
THROUGH
THE AGES

VOLUME I
FROM THE EARLIEST TIMES TO 1485

EDITED BY A. J. RODERICK

CHRISTOPHER DAVIES (PUBLISHERS) LTD.

First Impression: November 1959

Printed by
CAMBRIAN NEWS, ABERYSTWYTH

Published by
CHRISTOPHER DAVIES (PUBLISHERS) LTD.,
Publishers of *Llyfrau'r Dryw*,
LLANDYBIE, CARMARTHENSHIRE

FOREWORD

DURING the winter of 1958–59 a series of twenty-four twenty-minute talks was broadcast in the Welsh Home Service of the B.B.C. under the general title of *Wales through the Ages*. The talks traced the history of Wales from the earliest times to the end of the fifteenth century.

As the series progressed it became increasingly clear that there was an enthusiastic audience for the talks and that many people would like to have them available in print.

The present volume is the result. In it the twenty-four talks are reproduced very largely in the form in which they were broadcast. Minor verbal alterations have been made in some of the scripts, and sentences, and occasionally paragraphs, which had to be omitted in the broadcast owing to the exigencies of timing have been restored.

The titles and speakers were selected by a small advisory panel consisting of the following :—Dr. Thomas Parry, Principal of the University College of Wales, Aberystwyth, Professor Glyn Roberts of the University College of North Wales, Bangor, Professor David Williams of the University College of Wales, Aberystwyth, and the editor.

The talks were not intended to deal exhaustively with the history of Wales ; if that had been the aim they would have become a mere catalogue of facts. The aim was to select the main aspects of the history of Wales prior to the sixteenth century, and to invite experts to talk about them. It says much for the vigour of Welsh historical and allied studies that no fewer than twenty-two scholars have contributed to this series. Their contributions embody the results of much original thinking and research.

During the winter of 1959–60 a similar series of talks is to be broadcast on the Welsh Home Service, dealing with the history of Wales from the beginning of the sixteenth century to the present time.

CONTENTS

List of Illustrations

Acknowledgements

THE Editor and publishers gratefully acknowledge the permission given to reproduce the following illustrations :—

Frontispiece : David Jones, Esq., C.B.E.

Ill. No. 1 : Dr. J. K. St. Joseph, Selwyn College, Cambridge.

,, ,, 2 : Römisch-Germanisches, Zentralmuseum, Mainz.

,, ,, 3, 4 & 5 : The National Museum of Wales.

,, ,, 6 : Professor Stuart Piggott, The University, Edinburgh.

,, ,, 7 : H. Tempest, Ltd., Castle Street, Cardiff.

,, ,, 8 : Llew E. Morgan, Merton, Ystradgynlais.

,, ,, 9 : The National Library of Wales, Aberystwyth.

,, ,, 10 : Country Life Ltd., Tavistock Street, London, W.C.2.

,, ,, 11 : H. Turner, Esq., Fishguard.

The maps were drawn by Dr. Margaret Davies, Cardiff.

WALES THROUGH THE AGES

THE FIRST PEOPLE

By Glyn Daniel

WHEN we think about the history of Wales, most of us picture Wales before the Industrial Revolution as a green country of fields and hills, of small farms, villages and country towns. And so it was — an agricultural country whose wealth was based on crops and farmstock, whose fame abroad was based on mutton and cheese. But it was not always so. Just as there is a beginning to the Industrial Revolution in Wales so there was a beginning to the agricultural revolution — sometimes called the Neolithic Revolution — and this took place in Wales somewhere around 2000 B.C. That is to say, that about as many years before the birth of Christ as we are after, the first farmers settled in western Britain, and the first plots of wheat were cultivated, the first cows milked and sheep tended. Now of course the art and craft of agriculture had been discovered much earlier elsewhere ; there are farmers and fields in the Danube area at least as early as 4000 B.C., and in the Near East, where at least for the western world agriculture was discovered, there were peasant farmers as early as 7000 or 8000 B.C.

These dates are not guesswork. They are based on the new technique of Carbon 14 dating which was discovered by Professor Willard Libby in Chicago ten years ago as a by-product of research into nuclear physics. This extraordinary technique gives us accurate dates for thousands of years before the first dates were ever recorded by man himself, which were 3000 B.C. in Egypt and Mesopotamia. We can therefore now say with a fair degree of certainty that the first agriculturists got to Europe in the fourth millennium B.C. and eventually got to the British Isles between 2500 and 2000 B.C.

11

But the story of man in Wales does not begin then ; it does not begin with the first farmers. Man had been in Wales for thousands of years before that, living as a hunter and a fisher, and a collector of roots and berries. This is the first phase in Welsh history, the Food-Gathering Stage when man was, economically at least, a savage like the Eskimos or the Australian aborigines or the American Indians before Columbus. When did this phase begin — the phase which the archæologists call the Palæolithic and Mesolithic — the Old and Middle Stone Ages ? It began in Wales at least 50,000 years ago and possibly earlier, and it is a rather sobering thought that during the greater part of man's life in Wales he was a food-gatherer.

Do not suppose that there were ever many people in Wales in these long early millennia, and most probably there were often hundreds of years when no human beings lived in Britain at all, particularly when the ice sheets lay across the country and tundra vegetation grew on the windswept wastes of southern Britain. Our best evidence for these Palæolithic hunters in Wales comes from the rock-shelters or small caves in which the hunters lived, like Cae-gwyn cave near St. Asaph, or King Arthur's cave near Ross-on-Wye, Paviland in Gower, and Coygan in southern Carmarthenshire.

The Goat's Hole cave at Paviland in Gower is the best known, and the richest, cave in Wales. It was first excavated in 1823 by William Buckland, the Oxford geologist who later became dean of Westminster. He found, in addition to quantities of human tools and animal bones, the headless body of what is now thought to be a young man aged about twenty-five, but which Buckland thought to be a young woman : it is always known as the Red Lady of Paviland. With the burial were ivory rods and rings and many sea-shells ; the bones were stained with red ochre, and nearby was a complete elephant skull. This was a ceremonial burial, a careful ritual burial ; we find many of them from Palæolithic sites in France and Spain, and often they are covered with red ochre — perhaps because it was the colour of blood ? Who knows what ideas, what beliefs, caused such careful treatment of the dead ? We may well have in Paviland the very beginnings of some primitive form of religion.

What we do not have in Wales, or for that matter anywhere in the British Isles, is any painted or engraved caves. The great painted and engraved caves of France and Spain are well known, and places like Altamira and Lascaux, Font de Gaume and Niaux are our proudest heritage of man's earliest art. It has been suggested from time to time that Bacon's Hole in the Gower peninsula had some Palæolithic art on its walls but most people think the marks there are natural. Of course it is not impossible that we should find a Palæolithic painted and engraved cave in Wales — not impossible, but to most people unlikely.

From the animal bones in Paviland and elsewhere we can form a good idea of what these early men hunted — the wild horse, cave bear, wild ox, the woolly rhinoceros, reindeer, mammoth and hyena.

The Palæolithic hunters and their Mesolithic successors, who lived in Wales as the ice sheets retreated and present-day conditions began to come into existence, form an interesting but, it must be admitted, not a very exciting or relevant beginning to the main story of the past of Wales. Maybe the blood of some of these people still flows in our veins but they cannot have been an important ethnic element in the population of Wales. Nor, I think, do many of us find it easy to project our minds back and see these people living in caves and on coastal sites. We can, however, feel more direct contact with the first Neolithic people who arrived, as I have said, somewhere around 2000 B.C., probably from Gloucestershire and Wessex, with their knowledge of agriculture and pottery-making. We still know very little about the first farmers in Wales, these first Neolithic people, but in the last few years some of their houses have been found, by Mrs. Audrey Williams on St. David's Head for example, and by Dr. Savory at Stormy Down near Porthcawl.

What we do know a great deal about is the slightly later settlers who came by sea to Wales from western France and perhaps Spain, and who built the cromlechau that are such a feature of some parts of Wales, particularly Anglesey and Pembrokeshire. We know about these cromlech builders for the very obvious reason that they built these large, impressive and obvious stone tombs. There are between sixty and seventy of them surviving still in Wales. Sometimes they are in large mounds of earth and stones like the Tinkinswood cromlech near St. Nicholas, south of the road from Cardiff to Bridgend, or the Carneddau Hengwm in Merionethshire. At other times they stand completely free like the Pentre Ifan cromlech in Pembrokeshire.

We can distinguish different types among them — different tomb-plans, just as at the present day the Christian religion has different church-plans varying from Byzantine domed basilicas to rectangular Methodist chapels. The study of these plans shows us that some of the cromlech builders — those who settled in the Gower peninsula and Glamorgan and Monmouthshire and later spread up into the Black Mountains— were originally from southern Brittany and the lower Loire valley ; while others, like the builders of Bryn-celli-ddu and Barclodiad y Gawres in Anglesey, most probably came from Spain and Portugal. These two Anglesey monuments had carvings on their walls, carvings of spirals and lozenges and zigzags, and these designs are also found in similar contexts in Iberia. The designs themselves are stylized and schematized versions of a goddess figure — the Earth Mother Goddess of east Mediterranean archæology — because the ultimate inspiration of these cromlech builders and their ultimate home was the Aegean world of the eastern Mediterranean. Perhaps the builders of Bryn-celli-ddu and Barclodiad y Gawres did not come direct from Iberia to Wales ; they migrated across the Irish Sea to Anglesey, and in great Irish monuments like New Grange we find the exact prototypes for the plan and the art of the Anglesey monuments. We must admire the skill of these intrepid mariners who sailed along the western seaways of Atlantic Europe to Ireland and Wales, as also their skill in building their great stone tombs.

Why did they come to Ireland and Wales ? No one really knows ; but I think, and so do many other people, that they were prospecting. They were adventurers, explorers searching out new lands as Vasco da Gama and Columbus did much later. What they particularly were looking for in the British Isles was copper and tin, and I think they found these substances in Ireland and Cornwall and exported them back to the Mediterranean world. The cromlech builders may well have been the first metal-workers in the British Isles, but this is only an idea : what is certain is that they did not put objects of copper and tin, or of bronze (which was an alloy of copper and tin) in their tombs. But then do we put objects in our graves that would tell archæologists at once whether we belonged to the Stone Age, Bronze Age or Iron Age ? It is something to think about.

Did these cromlech builders also build circular temples of stone ? Are they also the builders of stone circles ? Are they, to put no finer point upon it, the people who built Stonehenge and Avebury in Wiltshire ?

Two things are certain. There are few stone circles in Wales, but they do exist. Secondly, some of the stones used in the construction of Stonehenge — the so-called ' blue stones ' — came at least 200 miles, from Pembrokeshire, from the Presely Mountains. This was proved beyond a shadow of doubt in the early nineteen-twenties by Dr. H. H. Thomas of the Geological Survey, working on an idea suggested to him by that great Welsh geologist, O. T. Jones. And that too is a most remarkable fact in the early history of Wales — the moving of a great number of stones from Presely to the Wiltshire Downs — a fine feat of transport engineering. There is no doubt that the cromlech builders were great men. They lived somewhere between 2000 B.C. and 1500 B.C. and are one of the formative elements in the ultimate population of Wales. Soon after the first cromlech builders had arrived there came from what is now England quite different people, called the Beaker people because of their custom of placing in their graves a small red-brown drinking cup from five to seven inches in height. The Beaker people buried their dead in single graves under round mounds, whereas the cromlech builders used to bury large numbers of people in their big stone tombs — as many as fifty or more : the cromlechs were essentially collective tombs used over a period of time by a village or family group.

We know nearly all of that little we do know in Wales about the people of the early second millennium B.C. from their tombs. Of their settlements we know almost nothing as yet, and it is a

strange thing that the people who could build the great cromlechau and transport stones from Pembrokeshire to Stonehenge
yet did not build, as far as we can make out, stone houses and
villages that have survived to the present day. Perhaps they
were largely pastoral and semi-nomadic in their economy ;
we do not know.

What we do know is that the cromlech builders and the
Beaker folk illustrate a feature of early Welsh history which
occurs time and time again. Wales looks two ways ; eastwards
to England and westwards and southwards to Ireland, Brittany
and Spain. This dichotomy of outlook, which geographers
like Professor Fleure and archæologists like Sir Cyril Fox would
call the dual aspect of the personality of Wales, is one of the
priceless and invigorating features of our early Welsh heritage.

But were these people Welsh — the hunters and fishers
who lived in caves near St. Asaph and Gower, the farmers in
their small houses at St. David's and Stormy Down, the men
who built the cromlechau, who buried their dead with pottery
beakers ?   It really depends on what we mean when we ask
the question, ' Were they Welsh ? ' They certainly lived in a
part of Britain which we today call Wales, so that they are the
first Welshmen in that sense. But did they speak Welsh or,
for that matter, any Celtic language ? This is a more difficult
question ;   we can say very little that is useful and reliable
about language if we have no written records, and there was no
written language in Wales before the Romans. Our pre-
Roman forbears, the ancient Britons, were illiterate. Therefore we can only guess at what they spoke, and use comparative
evidence. It is a fair guess that the people of the Late Bronze
Age and Early Iron Age were Celtic-speaking. And we know
of course that the language of the Britons when conquered by
the Romans was Ancient British — the language out of which
Welsh, and Breton, developed.

But the story which I have told you in the merest outline
ends 1,500 years before Caesar. I think it unlikely that any of
these people spoke a Celtic language, although just possibly
the Beaker folk might have been Indo-Europeans. The cromlech builders came from France and Spain and Portugal ; they
were Mediterranean folk, short dark people I expect, and

almost certainly they spoke a non-Indo-European language, a Mediterranean language perhaps akin to modern Berber, a language of north Africa, or even to the Basque language, spoken in southern France and northern Spain. But this is guesswork. What is not guesswork is that they were Mediterraneans.

Sir John Rhys, that great scholar of Wales and the Welsh, used to set out the early history of Wales in three great phases, which he called the pre-Iberian, the Iberian and the Celtic. It was a great over-simplification, as he would himself have been the first to admit if he had survived to study the modern archæological evidence. We have so far seen something of the first two phases of John Rhys, and Professor Grimes will take the story from 1500 B.C. to the Roman conquest; which was certainly the time of the coming of the Celts to Wales.

LATER PREHISTORY AND THE COMING OF THE CELTS

By W. F. Grimes

In prehistory it often happens that periods of intense activity are followed by periods of comparative quiet. The first half of the second millennium B.C. was a time of much movement, which was partly at least connected with the exploitation of the first metals. The following five hundred years were much quieter : a time of consolidation in which the new elements of the preceding phase were absorbed. By 1000 B.C. a large part of Britain, not merely Wales, possessed a Bronze Age culture which, whatever its local variations, was remarkably uniform in its general character.

Like all generalisations this is only a nearly-true statement. Its chief inaccuracy is that there was in fact one important influx of newcomers just as what we call the Middle Bronze Age was starting. These people came from roughly north-western France : their main groups crossed the English Channel to colonise Wessex, where they have been recognisable by a series of remarkably rich burials — burials containing objects of gold, amber and faience, as well as fine bronzes, which suggest that the people were of a wealthy aristocratic caste.

But although Wessex has given this culture its name it is not rigidly confined to Wessex ; and the manner of its occurrence in Wales is interesting because it illustrates a process which operated throughout the whole of Welsh prehistory. The Wessex Culture is represented in the coastal plain of Glamorgan in a number of the burial mounds that are common in certain parts of that area. The mounds themselves are elaborately constructed : they have walls or kerbs of stone enclosing the central burial area ; or sometimes circles of stakes, contained within the body of the mound, in which turf is often an important constituent. The burials are usually cremations in

18

which a quantity of imperfectly burnt bones is placed in a pit or in a pottery urn. The bones may be accompanied by objects of which perhaps the most intriguing are the small highly decorated cups called pigmy or incense cups, which are assumed to have served some ritual purpose. But stone and even bronze implements also occur and as a whole are of what archæologists call ' Wessex ' type.

The movement represented by these burials was not a large one, though for some centuries it coloured the Bronze Age of south Wales. What is particularly significant about it is that it shows the south coastal plain of Wales once again as a sort of extension of southern England, receiving influences from that direction which touched the rest of Wales slightly if at all. The ' Wessex ' burials are concentrated mainly in the Llantwit Major area of Glamorgan and perhaps the most outstanding example was one on Breach Farm, to the south-west of Cowbridge. There, beneath a typical ' composite ' barrow, was found a central burial-pit containing burnt bones with a remarkable series of flint implements, grooved stones for straightening arrowshafts, an early type of bronze axe, and a finely decorated pigmy cup. Particulary important are the cup, whose incised ornament still retains traces of the original red pigment with which it had been emphasised ; and the series of exquisitely worked barbed-and-tanged arrowheads, which call to mind at once the even finer arrowheads that accompany related burials in Brittany.

We know of practically no dwelling-sites of the Bronze Age. During this time, as at all other periods, a few caves were lived in and have produced a number of finds, of which perhaps the chief was the small hoard of bronze implements (including a rare example of a saw) from the cave known as Cat's Hole, near Monkton, Pembroke. But caves in Wales have a very limited distribution, being confined mainly to the Carboniferous Limestone ; and for the rest our knowledge of the period comes from the many chance discoveries of bronze and other implements — and especially from burials.

It is well known that as the megalithic chamber tombs (*cromlechau*) went out of use, and with them the practice of communal burial, round burial mounds, with individual burial, took their place. Such mounds could be elaborately constructed as with the Wessex barrows already described. They are a feature of many parts of the countryside, appearing as smooth earth mounds (barrows) in those areas of the low-land that were occupied by man and frequently as heaps of stone (cairns) on the hills.

In the burials themselves the significant thing is the change-over to cremation from the practice of inhumation which was usual in the Early Bronze Age. These cremated burials seldom have anything with the bones other than the pottery urn which contains them (where one occurs). But prehistoric pottery is very valuable as a pointer to contacts between cultures ; and many of these urns show in their shapes and ornament traces of influence from other parts of the country. In them we see the continuing tendency for different parts of Wales to look in different directions. In north Wales, for example, urns in Anglesey and the north-west display resemblances to those of Derbyshire and Yorkshire. On the other hand some urns look more towards Ireland. There have been several from central Wales in recent years in which Irish influence can be detected ; but Irish influence is by no means confined to one part of the country.

On the industrial side the people of the Middle Bronze Age developed the simple types of bronze implement and weapon used by their predecessors into more efficient forms which are evidence of a marked increase in technical skill and knowledge. It is impossible to go into detail about the many finds that have come to light, but by the end of the period axes, knives, spear-heads had reached a level of development which could not be surpassed except by some kind of revolutionary process ; and a few new types were beginning to appear as a sign that needs were becoming more complicated.

But this comparatively quiet period came to an end at about 1000 B.C. This was the Late Bronze Age — and again for about five hundred years there was unrest. The causes now were the economic and social disturbances which followed the first exploitation of European sources of iron, already in use on the Continent.

The first signs of change are the entirely new types of bronzes

that began to appear not so much as single finds but in hoards
— that is, collections of objects which had belonged to travell-
ing tradesmen or smiths. Hoards containing a few objects occur
in earlier phases of the Bronze Age, but they become much
more numerous and much larger in the Late Bronze Age and
are the first clear indication in Britain as a whole of the existence of a class of specialist metal-workers and traders. The
Late Bronze Age hoards, like the famous ones from Guilsfield in
Montgomeryshire, and Glan-cych on the border of Pembrokeshire and Carmarthenshire, may contain large numbers of
items and they will include broken and obsolete types and waste
metal as well as new products which were derived from continental forms if not actually made on the Continent. These
new forms were more efficient than their British counterparts,
good as many of them were, and their use became widespread.
Perhaps the commonest, if not the most distinctive, were the
heavy swords which replaced the native more delicately made
rapiers, and the socketed axes which were more efficiently
compact than the best native axes.

But through all this the natives continued in their old way.
They still cremated their dead and buried the remains in
barrows. Their urns, often crude and large — some are
eighteen inches or more in height — are derived directly from
the urns of previous periods.

But presently there were further changes. The new bronzes,
in the first place, take on a different character. Outstanding
amongst them is the famous hoard from Llyn Fawr in
Glamorgan. The hoard was found in 1912 when the lake was
being drained for conversion into a reservoir. In addition to
ordinary types it included comparatively rare articles like
harness-fittings, socketed sickles, razors, two large sheet-metal
cauldrons. But its outstanding feature is the presence in it of
objects of iron, the new metal : one a sickle, another a spearhead, the third a fragment of a sword. Obviously, then, the
Llyn Fawr hoard is at the turn from the Bronze to the Iron
Age — so much at the turn that the iron sickle and spearhead
have been produced by techniques which are suited to bronze
rather than to iron. On the other hand, the sword is purely
of the Iron Age : it is an unmistakeable product of the Hall-

statt culture, so called from Hallstatt, in Austria, the name-site of the first continental Iron Age.

Other objects of Hallstatt type are being found in Wales, both in hoards and as single finds ; but however they came, and from whatever direction, the Llyn Fawr series as a whole certainly looks like the equipment of a settlement. An Irish origin for many of its objects also seems pretty certain : they constitute a reminder that the earlier trade with Ireland (and other parts of the British Isles) continued. Further support for the conclusion that some of these later finds are a mark of settlement of new peoples is provided by the growing number of finds of pottery of types which on general evidence would be dated to the centuries just after 1000 B.C. Some of this material resembles the vessels that are found in the Late Bronze Age cemeteries of southern and eastern England, though no such cemeteries have yet been recorded in Wales. Some of it, referred to below, has unmistakeable resemblances to the pottery of the British version of the first Iron Age. It is, in fact, very difficult to separate the different parts of what was evidently a continuing and complicated process throughout the period of the change from bronze to iron. The one certain inference to be drawn is that during this time, and particularly towards the end of it, Wales received some of the newcomers who were now appearing in Britain, traders and settlers alike.

At the same time the traditional links with Ireland and other lands round the Irish Sea during this period were not only those of trade. The most important folk-movement is represented by a highly distinctive type of pottery burial-urn, known as the ' encrusted urn ' because of the use made of strips of clay in its decoration to give a raised or encrusted effect. Its story is an interesting one. It seems to have started with a comparatively simple form in the north of England, and the idea seems to have travelled anti-clockwise into Ireland and so back across the Irish Sea into Wales. Encrusted urns have been found in Anglesey, Flintshire, Cardiganshire, Carmarthenshire and Pembrokeshire. The Flintshire example is of an early type which was no doubt derived directly from the north of England. The others are later in the development and mark the end of the process. But both show that the connexion of Wales with other parts of the Highland Zone of western and northern Britain were never really broken.

Some time after 500 B.C. the Bronze Age finally gave way to the Iron Age. The iron-using people came to Britain in three main invasions and there is a growing amount of evidence to show that all three are represented in Wales. Iron Age A, so-called, is a composite culture which is really the British version of the first continental Iron Age referred to earlier, though it is inevitably a good deal later than its continental fore-runners. Its pottery is frequently ornamented in a distinctive manner with finger-nail or finger-tip impressions. It is beginning to present itself both in north and in south Wales, as well as along the English-Welsh border ; and while it has not yet occurred in large quantities it is quite similar to that found elsewhere in these islands.

Iron Age B, the equivalent of the continental Iron Age named from La Tène in Switzerland, appears in an advanced form in Gower, in the south-eastern coastal plain, and again in the border counties. Some of the pottery looks very like that made and used in south-western England in the first century B.C., but the movements that brought these people were complicated. More widely distributed are a number of examples of the fine decorated metal work which is the chief element in what is called ' Celtic art' : objects like the tankard from Trawsfynydd in the Liverpool Museum ; the bronze collar from Llandysul, now at Bristol ; and, above all, the great hoard of objects of bronze and iron from Llyn Cerrig Bach, in Anglesey, in the National Museum of Wales. This last dis-covery is one of the most important ever to have been made. It included harness-fittings, shield-ornaments and other decorative pieces as well as weapons and parts of chariots. The collection, which is of very mixed origins, seems to represent a succession of votive offerings made over a couple of centuries. Here, if anywhere, are indications of the Druidic religion which made Anglesey notorious to the Romans. It is significant that the latest object in the hoard belongs to the time when the Romans put an end to Anglesey as a centre of the Druidic cult in 61 A.D.

There can be little doubt that many of the hill forts of Wales belong to this second phase of the pre-Roman Iron Age, though there is at present little direct evidence about them. Their distribution shows how the people who built and lived in them colonised the country. On the east, penetration took place up the Severn Valley and its tributaries. Here and in the marginal hills of Denbighshire and Flintshire in the north there are many so-called forts (they are really defended settlements) in dominant positions. Many have elaborate defences which are of similar type to those in the south of England. From the few which have been excavated the results have been far from simple. In some there has been much rebuilding and reconstruction of the defences, but they produce very little in the way of finds by which the various changes can be dated. Others yield pottery of different cultural groups, suggesting that several influences were at work — including some which may well have come across England from the east and north-east.

On the west earthworks of one sort or another are more numerous and many of them are less certainly prehistoric. They are often quite small, though they may have quite strong defences. But bigger forts also occur and there are some fine ones in the Vale of Glamorgan and also in Caernarfonshire. The pattern of distribution for the country as a whole shows that these hill fort builders were content to occupy dominant positions along the valleys or near them. They do not appear to have concerned themselves with the upland areas, which may well have continued to carry the remnants of the Bronze Age population.

Finally, what British archæologists call Iron Age C means the Belgae. The Belgae were people of mixed Celtic and Teutonic stock who were establishing their kingdoms in southeastern England in the first century B.C. There are hints of them in Monmouthshire and elsewhere in the border counties, and they were certainly expanding steadily westwards ; but it is perhaps not yet certain whether their presence so far west was due to flight from the Roman armies or to tribal expansion. In any case the movement ended with the appearance of Roman troops in Wales before 50 A.D.

It remains to consider how the coming of the Celts fits into this fifteen hundred years of complicated colonisations and trade-movements. In trying to answer this question the archæologist is confronted with the basic difficulty that the

Celts were people who spoke a certain language (or group of languages) while the evidence of archæology is things, which in the absence of writing, give no clue to language at all.

It is nevertheless possible to work backwards through these things ; and with their help to trace connexions between the earliest peoples whose language is known and those whose language can be inferred. From the statements of Greek travellers it is known that by the sixth century B.C. the British Isles had names that appear to be Celtic : the linguistic experts must decide whether they are indeed Celtic. Archæologically the indications are that in Britain and elsewhere in the west the coming of the Celts must be equated with some or all of those movements that spanned the change-over from the Bronze to the Iron Age in the early part of the first millennium B.C. Certainly the Iron Age A people should be accepted as Celts and it may be that some of the Late Bronze Age peoples were Celtic also. The hope of a more definite answer (if indeed one can be found by archæological means) hangs on further investigation of the hill forts and other settlements, about which at present all too little is known.

ROMAN WALES

By Donald Moore

WE have already seen what a long and complex story can now be told about the prehistoric past of man in Wales through archæological studies. The present topic brings us to the beginning of the historic period, in the sense that we can obtain at least some of our knowledge from written evidence.

Two thousand years ago a great empire had been established around the shores of the Mediterranean sea by the Romans. It embraced all continental Europe south of the rivers Rhine and Danube, much of. Asia Minor, all Egypt, and the north African coast. It was governed by autocratic emperors, defended by highly trained armies of professional soldiers, and administered by military commanders and higher civil servants recruited from the best Roman families. Latin was the official language, and everyone of significance could read and write. Gold, silver and bronze coins were in circulation. Farming, manufacturing and mining were conducted on a large scale, and trade flourished. Throughout the provinces there were well planned cities with public buildings, temples, shops and houses built of stone. Arterial roads led from Rome to the farthest frontiers.

North-west of this empire lay the island of Britain. There, tribes of warlike people lived in fortified encampments on hill-tops in a thickly wooded countryside. In the shelter of their earth and timber strongholds they built their round wooden houses with thatched roofs. Women would sit at doorways making crude pottery from local clay or spinning woollen yarn with the aid of distaff and spindle-whorl. Herds and flocks provided beef and mutton to eat, and corn was grown in places. Milk, beer, and probably mead, were drunk. The menfolk were both farmers and warriors ; they loved brightly coloured clothes ; many had skill in making swords and spears of iron,

26

1.   Old Oswestry Hill Fort

2. A Model of a Roman Soldier

or harness fittings and personal adornments of bronze. In battle they used blue war-paint to terrify their enemies ; some fought on foot, others in chariots. Politically they existed in small independent tribal units, except in south-east Britain, where petty kingdoms had begun to develop. There, too, a gold coinage had been introduced. The people had their own pantheon of gods and heroes. Their priests were called Druids, and they wielded great influence. They taught a doctrine involving the transmigration of souls, and conducted human sacrifices.

In 43 A.D. the Romans decided to invade Britain. The emperor Claudius assembled a force of 50,000 fighting men at Boulogne. They crossed the Channel by night and landed on the Kentish coast. Stiff fighting followed. When victory was in sight the emperor himself arrived to claim his share of the honours.

Why should the Romans have been attracted to this remote island ? In general, Roman military experts wanted to find the ultimate defensible frontier for the Empire. Politicians and merchants were interested in economic resources. Britain was already known to be a source of slaves, hunting dogs and grain, and it contained deposits of gold, silver and other metals. Pearls could be found in its coastal waters. And now the emperor Claudius, eager for military glory, had learned that the great Cymbeline, king of south-east Britain, had died, and that his sons were quarrelling over the future of the kingdom. There was a risk that an anti-Roman government might be set up.

Within four years most of south-east Britain was in Roman hands. But north-west of a line joining the Trent and the lower Severn, a stiffer opposition and more difficult terrain was encountered. A British prince from the lowland, named Caradog, or Caratacus, set about organising the resistance of free tribes in what is now Wales. But he was captured and sent to Rome.

Fighting in Wales and the border country continued for some thirty years. Native hill forts were stormed, captured and dismantled ; Roman forts were established at strategic points. Anglesey was a particular source of resistance ; it was the headquarters of the Druids, whose cult was obnoxious to the Romans.

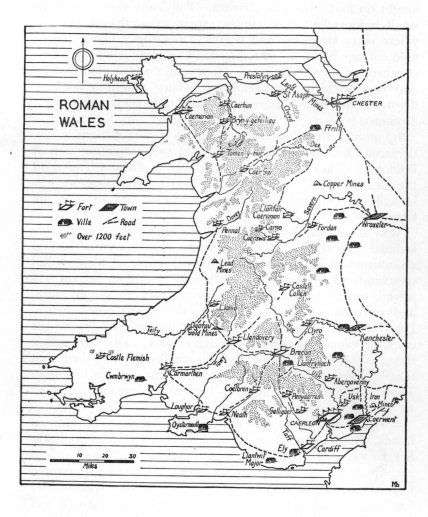

The Roman historian Tacitus describes the scene as the Roman soldiers formed up with their landing craft on the south shore of the Menai Straits. The enemy line was drawn up on the opposite bank. The British warriors were armed to the teeth and womenfolk darted among their ranks with blazing torches, their hair dishevelled and their garments fluttering like shrouds. The Druids roundabout lifted their hands to heaven and declaimed fearful curses. The Romans were terrified, but, urged on by their general, they pressed home their attack. The Druids and their adherents were massacred, the sacred groves of oak burned down.

The story of the conquest is exciting, because we have written accounts of events and personalities. But for a deeper knowledge of the Roman occupation we have to turn to the archæological record. Nearly fifty years ago Professor Haverfield read to the Honourable Society of Cymmrodorion his paper on " Military Aspects of Roman Wales." It was the most important account of its kind up to that time. Since then our knowledge has been greatly increased by many investigators, but notably by Sir Mortimer Wheeler and the late Doctor Nash-Williams.

By the year 75 A.D. Wales had been finally brought under Roman control. It was dominated by two legionary fortresses, Caerleon and Chester, one at either extremity of the border. Caerleon was named *Isca*, a word akin to the river-name Usk. Chester, on the river Dee, was similarly called *Deva*. Each fortress held nearly six thousand legionaries — heavily-armed and well-paid foot soldiers. The whole of Wales became a frontier zone. Some twenty-four field forts were built at strategic points and linked by hundred of miles of specially laid roads.

The route between Chester and Caerleon avoided the mountains and traversed the lowlands of the border. The main road west from Caerleon followed the coastal plain for most of its length and terminated at *Moridunum*, a fort situated where Carmarthen now stands. Along the north coast the main road from Chester ran to Caernarfon, then called *Segontium*. Milestones found along the course of these roads testify to their importance. The chief inland forts were the

Brecon Gaer, the Forden Gaer and Caersws. In most cases the modern Welsh place-name has preserved the memory of the former fortification.

Each of these field forts was garrisoned by auxiliary troops, who were paid and equipped on a lower scale than the legionaries. The nominal strength of a fort was either five hundred cavalry or a thousand infantry. But after about fifty years' intensive occupation many forts were left in charge of small holding units or even abandoned, until some crisis obliged the Romans to reinforce their garrisons. Fragments of building inscriptions identify some of those stationed in Wales : there were *Vettones* from Spain at Brecon, *Nervii* from north-east France at Caer Gai near Bala, and Asturians from north-west Spain at Llanio in Cardiganshire.

The auxiliary forts were the most conspicuous evidence of Roman rule in Wales. Each fort was laid out according to a standard pattern. A rampart of earth surrounded by a ditch was dug round a rectangular area of about five acres, shaped like a playing card. The rampart would often be faced with stone, and furnished with a crenellated parapet and stone turrets. Inside the fort, streets were laid out in chequerboard pattern. The chief buildings, grouped in the centre, consisted of the headquarters, the commanding officer's residence, and the granary. These were usually built of stone and roofed with tiles. The rest of the enclosure would contain rows of long timber barrack blocks, storerooms, stables, workshops, and a hospital. Four roads led out through arched gateways from the middle of each side of the fort. Outside lay the bath block, and probably a cluster of traders' booths.

A legionary fortress was very much larger, covering about fifty acres. The site of the fortress of *Deva* is largely obscured by the present-day city of Chester. But *Isca* is only partly covered by the streets of Caerleon. Much excavation has been done there, especially by archæologists from the National Museum of Wales. Beneath the meadows encircled by the river Usk have been discovered remains of stone-built barrack blocks, administrative buildings, ovens for cooking food, and stretches of stone-faced rampart. Outside the fortress is a spectacular structure, the amphitheatre. This was a large oval arena, open to the sky, and surrounded by high banks sloping inwards. Here the soldiers would watch entertainments or military demonstrations. Between the fortress and the river was a large civil settlement. Here lived traders, soldiers' families, and, no doubt, some of the native Celts from their hill-top fort at Lodge Wood nearby.

The romanization of native peoples was part of official policy. Tacitus records that as early as 80 A.D. young Britons of the upper classes were assiduously learning the Latin language, wearing the Roman toga, and taking Turkish-style baths. Towns with limited self-government were founded, and their councils were encouraged to raise funds for the erection of law courts, market places and baths.

The only true town founded in Roman Wales was at Caerwent. Its name, *Venta Silurum*, means, ' the market of the Silures'. It was a regional capital. Now why was it established here ? Firstly, the site was close to the fully romanized lowland. Secondly, it was in an area already well populated. Thirdly, the terrain and climate were less inhospitable than in the mountainous west. The Romans were a Mediterranean people, accustomed to clear skies and hot sunshine for much of the year. They must have been disappointed in the climate of western Britain.

About two-thirds of *Venta* have been excavated. Some foundations are still exposed ; impressive stretches of the town walls are still visible, standing in parts to a height of fifteen feet. The streets of the town were laid out in the familiar chequerboard plan. The main road from Caerleon to Gloucester ran through the middle of the town, past splendid public buildings. There were temples to Roman and Celtic gods. Shops fronted on the streets, with long narrow dwellings behind. On the outskirts were large houses set in ample grounds, and equipped with central heating, private baths and indoor sanitation. *Venta* was not a large town compared with others in the province ; its area was $44\frac{1}{2}$ acres, as against 170 for that prosperous mid-border town of *Viroconium* near modern Shrewsbury. The probable remains of a basilica-type church at Caerwent provide the only archæological evidence for Christianity in Roman Wales.

There are other traces of civil life in Wales, though almost confined to the south coastal plain. Villas, or country houses, with estates attached, were built in sheltered sites ; two examples have been excavated, at Llantwit Major and Ely in Glamorgan. Finds of tile and pottery elsewhere suggest the existence of more villas or at least romanized farmsteads. The occupants of villas were probably romanized Britons.

Some villas and forts were also connected with the development of mineral deposits. Lead was mined in the areas of Flintshire, Shropshire, Monmouthshire and Plynlimon. Copper was worked in the Parys mine in Anglesey, on Great Orme's Head, and on Llanymynech Hill near Oswestry. There were iron mines in the Forest of Dean, and gold mines at Dolau Cothi in Carmarthenshire. Deposits of clay were exploited to meet the demand for roofing tiles and coarse pottery.

The sea routes must have been important along the north and south coasts of Wales. Little evidence can be found for Roman shipping in British waters ; the Romans liked to travel by land. But they had obviously taken care to site many of their forts on navigable rivers and estuaries. They could, for example, have transported cargoes of pottery and tiles from the kilns of the Twentieth Legion at Holt by ship down the Dee to the coast, and thence around the isle of Anglesey to Caernarfon. A Roman merchantman sailing at about four knots would take from four to five days on such a voyage. Finds of building stone from Bath at Caerleon and Caerwent imply voyages across the Bristol Channel.

Control of the western sea approaches became vital from the mid-third century onwards. The Romans were now on the defensive. They were menaced by Irish raiders in the west, and also by Picts in the north and Saxons in the east and south. As countermeasures, new officials were appointed ; special forts were built near the coast, and naval units based on them. In Wales one such fort was constructed on the Taff at Cardiff on an earlier Roman site ; a smaller one was built at Holyhead in Anglesey. The old fort at Caernarfon was brought into use again, and at Caerwent the town wall was strengthened with bastions.

Sign of unrest and disorder were also evident within the Empire. Provincial generals and officials found that they could

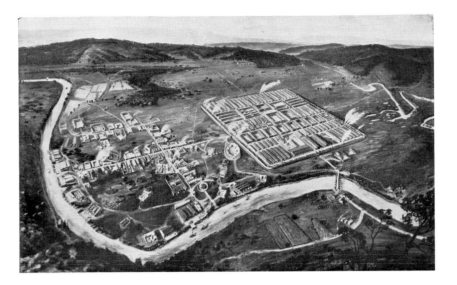

3. Caerleon in Roman times

4. A corner of the fort at Caerleon

5. The Roman Town at Caerwent

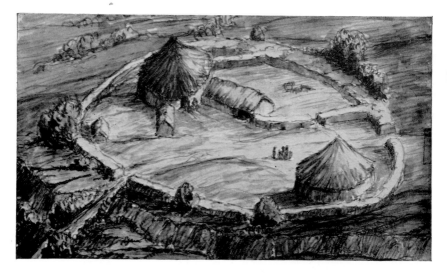

6. A Farm in Anglesey in the Sixth Century

seize control of provinces and even claim the imperial purple. On several occasions Britain was drained of fighting men and left open to barbarian attack. In 383 A.D. a Spanish-born commander, Magnus Maximus, established himself as ruler of Britain, France and Spain. But five years later he was defeated and killed in Italy. He somehow made a great impression on the inhabitants of Wales ; he figures in Welsh legend as Macsen Wledig, a king of Rome, who was impelled by a marvellous dream to journey across mountain and sea to a fort at Aber Sein in Arfon, where he was to meet his future wife. Her name, Helen, has been commemorated in many stretches of Roman road, known to this day as Sarn Helen. Maximus and his family were Christians. Their descendants were influential in Wales long after Roman times. Archæological evidence tells us nothing directly about Maximus in Wales. Only a few coins, pottery, or other objects that can be ascribed to later than 380 A.D. have been found in the Welsh military stations. This suggests that after Maximus effective Roman control of Wales ceased.

What had happened to the native population during the three-hundred-odd years of Roman occupation ? Evidence now coming to light increasingly suggests that they returned to their old hill forts, and even built new ones, presumably with Roman permission. There they lived much in their former way, but accepting some of the portable benefits of Roman civilisation, such as fine pottery dishes, glass bottles, bronze saucepans, mirrors and brooches. In parts of north Wales a new type of walled settlement appears, incorporating both rectangular and round buildings, built mostly of dry stone-work. One existed at Rhostryfan in Caernarfonshire, another at Dinllugwy in Anglesey. At the latter site Roman pottery seems to have been so prized that it was mended with iron rivets when broken. Hilltop fortifications at Tre'r Ceiri and Dinorben in north Wales, and at Dinas Powis and Llancarfan in south Wales, were also inhabited during the Roman period.

The Roman occupation was essentially an interlude, and yet something of the legacy of Rome can be detected in the growth of the Welsh language and literature, and in the political arrangements of the Dark Ages.

THE DAWN OF THE WELSH LANGUAGE

By Kenneth Jackson

PEOPLE sometimes ask me, " How old is the Welsh language ?" What do we mean by this question ? We all know that languages are not unchangeably fixed, but constantly evolve from one generation to the next, though nowadays this process is very slow because of the conservative influence of education and print. But most languages have gone through stages when this evolution has been fairly quick, often so much so that a new language has come into being by the comparatively rapid and complete breakdown of an older one. It is a familiar fact that French is a language which arose in this way out of the colloquial Latin spoken in France during the Roman Empire. Somewhere between about the sixth century and the ninth, the Latin spoken there changed to such an extent that it ceased to be any longer recognisably Latin, and by the ninth century we can speak of the French language as having already come into existence, in a very archaic form.

In exactly the same way Welsh is the product of a linguistic evolution, an even more rapid one, out of an older language — the one we call British. British was the speech of the ancient Britons of this island, both before the Roman occupation and during it ; the Britons were the direct ancestors of the modern Welsh people, and their language the direct ancestor of Welsh.

We do not know a great deal about British since there are no written British texts : the language of literature in Roman Britain was of course Latin. However a certain amount survives in the form of names of British people and places mentioned by classical authors, or in Roman official documents and Latin inscriptions of the Roman period ; and from these we can get a fair idea of some of its features. We can see that it must have been a language in much the same stage of evolution as Latin was. For instance, Latin nouns always end with a

34

case-termination, a final syllable which shows in what relation
the noun stands to the rest of the sentence ; a common form
with Latin masculine nouns is nominative ending in -*us*,
accusative in -*um*, genitive in -*ī*, and dative in -*ō*. It was the
same in British, indeed very closely so. Take the British name
Cunobelinos, the famous king of south-east Britain at the time of
the Roman conquest, from which comes the Welsh name
Cynfelyn. When it was the subject of the verb it was *Cunobelinos;*
when object, *Cunobelinon* ; when it meant " of Cunobelinos" it
was *Cunobelini*, and when " to Cunobelinos " it was *Cunobeli nu* —
all very like Latin *Virgilius*, accusative *Virgilium*, genitive
Virgilii, and dative *Virgilio*. But this is totally unlike Welsh,
of course. Or again, Latin nouns are sometimes made up of
two words joined together with a linking-vowel, like *agricola*,
" farmer," which is from *agr* -, " field ," a linking-vowel -*i*-,
and *colo*, " to cultivate." In just the same way *Cunobel inos* is a
compound of *cun*-, " hound", a linking-vowel -*o*-, and *Belinos*,
the name of a god. Here then are two of the many features
which show that British was a language whose form and construction was not very dissimilar to Latin. The same was true
of its pronunciation. All this made it easy for the Britons to
borrow many Latin words into their language during the
Romano-British period, with the result that Welsh today has
numerous Latin words in it which go right back to the spoken
Latin of the Roman Empire. For example, though British
must have had a native word for " fish," it also borrowed the
Latin word *piscis* — why, we do not know. Later the native
word, whatever it was, must have gone out of use, but the Latin
one still survives as the Welsh *pysg*.

Now I can give an answer to the question asked at the
beginning, " How old is Welsh ? " After the disappearance
of the Roman adminstration in Britain early in the fifth century,
the rate of linguistic change seems to have increased ; the
language was becoming " corrupted," as it were, perhaps as a
consequence of the social upheavals that must have been taking
place. This stage we call Late British. During the course of
the early sixth century this process became a landslide ; the
old language rapidly crumbled, very likely owing to the
intensification of social chaos arising from the Anglo-Saxon

attacks on Britain. By the second half of the sixth century a stage of comparative equilibrium had been reached, and a new language was born ; Welsh, known in this very ancient stage as Primitive Welsh. So the answer to our question is, " Welsh is as old as the middle of the sixth century."

This is a point of great importance to literature, because on it there depends the question whether the historical poems attributed to the late sixth century poets Taliesin and Aneirin can really have been composed in their time and by them, or whether they are forgeries. It used to be argued that Welsh did not yet exist so early as the sixth century, and therefore that these poems cannot be genuine. Hence the traditional name of these and some other contemporary poets, the Cynfeirdd, the " first poets," is very appropriate. They must have been among the first to write poetry in what was now Welsh.

Let me say something now about the nature of these drastic changes which turned British into Welsh in so short a time. I mentioned just now the final case-terminations of British names, and the linking-vowels joining the two elements of compound words, quoting *Cunobelinos* as an example. During the first half of the sixth century these final syllables and linking-vowels all disappeared, giving us in this instance the modern name Cynfelyn. It was this more than anything else which changed the whole appearance of British, and is responsible for the big difference between British and Welsh. The result was catastrophic, because with the loss of final syllables the language lost its entire system of case-endings, and it was now no longer possible to express these grammatical relations in this way. Exactly the same happened to Latin ; French has lost all the Latin case-endings, and both Welsh and French now have recourse to the use of prepositions and other means of compensating for it. Only a few traces survive in Welsh, for instance the preposition *erbyn*, " opposite, against." This is a compound of *ar* in the sense of " opposite " and *penn*, " end", meaning literally " opposite the end" ; the reason why it is *erbyn* instead of *arben* is that *pynn* here is a survival of the old dative case of *penn*. Occasionally, too, case-forms have lived because they were taken for separate words. So, there was a British name *Maglocu* of which the genitive was *Maglocunos* ;

when the case system broke down these became taken for two quite different names, and they have become in Welsh respectively *Meilyg* and *Maelgwn*.

Another important change is that called the soft mutation. In some languages a consonant between two vowels tends to be slackly pronounced. A well-known instance is the way a *-t-* between vowels is pronounced in American English as a *d*, in words like *beauty* pronounced *beaudy*. This happened in Late British in a very thorough-going way, affecting most of the consonants between vowels ; so that the British name *Caratacos* became *Caradagos*, whence *Caradog*. But it went still further. When two words came together in a construction closely linking them, such as a noun followed by an adjective, the first consonant of the second word was soft-mutated if the preceding word ended in a vowel, because it now stood between vowels just as much as if it had been in the interior of the word. Take British *merca teca*, " a pretty girl," both words ending in the feminine termination *-a*. Here the *t* in *teca* is as much between vowels as the *t* in *beauty* is, even though it is in a separate word. Consequently the *t* was soft-mutated, as also was the *c* of course. Hence we have the Welsh *merch deg*, " a pretty girl ". But if the preceding word did not end in a vowel in British the mutation did not take place, because the first consonant of the second word was not between vowels. So in British *marcos tecos*, " a handsome horse", where both words end in the masculine termination *-os*, the *t* did not come between vowels and was consequently not mutated ; hence Welsh *march teg*. This is the origin of the Welsh rule that an adjective is soft-mutated if it follows a feminine noun but not if it follows a masculine one. This has nothing to do with " euphony" ; *merch deg* is no more euphonious than *march teg*, and it would be a queer language that demanded euphony with the one gender and not with the other.

As Late British passed into Primitive Welsh many other changes occurred, and further ones during the later evolution of Primitive Welsh. Unfortunately we have no Primitive Welsh texts, any more than British, and have to rely largely on the same kind of evidence — names of people and places in Latin texts, inscriptions, and so on. But now we have an invaluable new source. During the Anglo-Saxon occupation of

Britain, which coincided with the Late British and Primitive Welsh periods, the English settlers borrowed a large number of place-names from the Britons. Thereafter the form of these names remained fixed, or changed only in accordance with the evolution of Anglo-Saxon, no longer with that of Welsh. These are therefore a kind of linguistic fossil, and they give us many precious indications as to what Welsh was like at a fairly date-able period. So, we know that Welsh words beginning with *h*- began with *s*- in British, or, to put it differently, that British *s*- at the beginning of a word has become Welsh *h*-. Take the river-name Severn. This was *Sabrina* in British and has become *Hafren* in Welsh. Now, it is clear that when the English settlers were getting near the Severn and learned its name, which must have happened during the later sixth century, the British *s*- must still have been an *s*-, or at any rate something between *s*- and *h*- which sounded to English ears like *s*-. Other-wise, if the name had already become Hafren they would have adopted it as *Hevern*, not *Severn*. This shows how immensely valuable the evidence of place-names borrowed from Welsh into English can be in fixing approximate dates for the sound-changes of the developing Welsh language.

Another instance of this kind is the Welsh *coed*, " wood." There is evidence that in the Primitive Welsh period the *oe* sound must have been a long *ē*, therefore *cēd*. This *cēd* occurs commonly in English place-names, in the form *chet*, with English *ch* for *c* ; so Chatham, which means " Wood Village" ; Chetwood is " Wood Wood", the first element Welsh and the second English. English place-names do not show the later stage *coed*, which means that *ē* did not become *oe* until the Anglo-Saxon occupation was complete. A second case of Welsh *oe* appearing in names as Primitive Welsh *ē* is *moel*, "bare hill", which was Primitive Welsh *mel*. This is seen in the Eng-lish *Melchet*, " the Wood by the Bare Hill" ; *Melrose*, " the Moor by the Bare Hill", with Welsh *rhos*, " moor " ; and *Malvern*, Welsh *moelfryn*, " the bare hilltop."

British had a *w*- sound at the beginning of words which became in later Welsh *gw*- ; so the British town-name *Venta* became Welsh Gwent. This had not yet happened during the Anglo-Saxon occupation, and British place-names keep the *w-* in English, not *gw-*. So, for example, the Romano-British town of *Venta Belgarum* in Hampshire is now Win-chester, " the Town of Went," not Gwinchester.

On the other hand a sound-change which had already occurred and does therefore appear in English place-names is that by which in certain instances an *u* became an *o*, as in Welsh *trom*, the feminine of *trwm*. This is seen in the name *Dover*. In the Roman period this was *Dubrae*, obviously related to Welsh *dwfr*, " water ", and meant " the waters ", referring to the streams there ; but by the time the English arrived this had already become *Dovr*, with *u* becoming *o* and soft-mutation of *-b*.

Everyone must have noticed how common the Welsh word *penn* is in English place-names, in the sense of " hill " or "end." This is true from Cornwall to Scotland. The Roman settlement of *Pennocrucium* in Staffordshire consists of British *pennos*, " hill," and *croucos*, " mound", whence Welsh *penn* and *crug* ; the name means therefore " the hilly mound." In Welsh it would be *Penngrug* ; in English it has become *Penkridge*. Another is *Penrith* in Cumberland, a compound of *penn* and *rhyd*, "ford," meaning therefore " at the end of the ford" ; and very similar is *Penpont* in Dumfriesshire, obviously meaning " at the end of the bridge." *Pencaitland* in East Lothian is Welsh *penn*, *oood*, and *llann* in its early meaning of " enclosure " or rather, it is *penn* and *coedlann* " wooded enclosure, copse", so that the name means " the end of the copse."

A very large number of such British place-names were adopted in English throughout the Primitive Welsh period, and they are found in all parts of England, even as far east as Dover. It is true that they are rather scarce in eastern England, and much commoner in the west, which was settled much later and probably more thinly. At any rate some Britons must clearly have survived the conquest or they could not have communicated these names to the English ; the pattern of place-names suggests they were comparatively few in the east and comparatively many in the west. Certainly the degree of Welsh blood in the English people must be considerable in many areas, notably Cumberland, the Welsh marches, and the west country.

Primitive Welsh continued to evolve, though the rate of evolution slowed down after the sixth century. With the latter part of the eighth century the earliest Welsh written texts begin, and for the first time Welsh becomes a written language in the modern sense, though unfortunately very little of it survives. This new period is called now not Primitive Welsh but Old Welsh, and it lasted until the middle of the twelfth century. The language did not change much during the Old Welsh period, nor has it changed a very great deal since ; the one great and drastic period of change came with the appearance of Primitive Welsh in the sixth century, and after that the progress of evolution has been much slower. This means that a text in Old Welsh need not necessarily be entirely unintelligible to a modern Welshman even though he has not studied the early language, as a text in Anglo-Saxon is unintelligible to a modern Englishman who has not studied Anglo-Saxon. It is true that the spelling of Old Welsh is so different from that of present-day Welsh that it would look meaningless to the modern non-specialist Welsh reader, but this is a matter of spelling, and if it is read aloud, correctly pronounced, Old Welsh need not always be so difficult to follow. Here for instance is the opening sentence of the Old Welsh document which sets out the rights and privileges of the church of St. Teilo at Llandaff (read somewhat as it must have been pronounced at the time) :—

> Lymma y cymreith ha bryein eccluys Teliau o Lanntaf a rodes breenhined hinn ha touyssocion Cymry yn trycyguidaul dy eccluys Teliau hac hir escip oll gueti ef, amcytarnedic o audurdaut papou Rumein.

It does not, I think, need any special knowledge of early Welsh to know that this means, " This is the ordinance and the prerogative of the church of Teilo of Llandaff which these kings and princes of Wales gave in perpetuity to the church of Teilo and to all the bishops after him, confirmed by the authority of the popes of Rome." The language is by now unquestionably Welsh, as any speaker of Welsh will recognise.

The history of Welsh is a fascinating subject, not only at the periods I have described but also the succeeding stages called Middle and Modern Welsh ; and the development of the dialects is full of interest too.   But, I think, the most absorbing part of all is these centuries of change after the collapse of Roman rule and during the course of the English occupation ; partly because the linguistic history of these centuries has so much to tell us about the political history of Britain and the relations between the English and the Welsh, more than at any other time in the long course of the Welsh language.

EARLY WELSH LITERATURE

By J. E. Caerwyn Williams

IT MAY not be generally true that the evil that men do lives after them and that the good is often interred with their bones, but it is true of Maelgwn Gwynedd, son of Cadwallon Lawhir, for of this powerful ruler who bore sway over north-west Wales in the second quarter of the sixth century A.D., we should know very little, had not his manifold sins attracted the fierce diatribes of Gildas, that most embittered preacher and monk of traditionalist views, in a Latin book which has outlived the ravages of time.

Writing, as he was, to convict lay and ecclesiastical rulers of sin and of responsibility for the ruin of Britain, Gildas could not have passed over in silence Maelgwn Gwynedd's misdeeds. But these, though they are numerous and colourful, do not make very interesting reading today, and we should have been far more grateful had we been told more about his attainments and achievements. However, Gildas was in no mood to commend Maelgwn ; indeed, one of his indictments of the prince was that he was altogether too fond of tributes of praise ! He did not listen to Christ's followers, that is, the clergy, singing the praises of God, but he lent a ready ear to praise of himself : he heard what Gildas describes as " the voice of the rascally crew yelling forth, like bacchanalian revellers, full of lies and foaming phlegm, so as to besmear every one near them."

Unfortunately, it is not as easy for us as for sixth century readers to identify this " rascally crew " who sang the praises of Maelgwn Gwynedd. But we know that the Celts of these islands, both British and Irish, had, like the Celts of the Continent, bards who sang songs of eulogy and satire, and it does not require much exercise of the imagination to see in Gildas's most uncomplimentary description of these panegyrists in Maelgwn Gwynedd's court a reference not to individual sycophants but to members of the bardic order, surely one of the earliest references to bards on Welsh soil. As we shall see, these bards also told stories and sagas ; and as Gildas elsewhere in his book castigates his fellow clerics for listening to the scandalous tales of men of the world, we may quite legitimately, I think, conclude that Gildas's prejudice was great enough for him to regard the bards' singing as yelling and their enthusiasm as bacchanalian revelry.

We may do so with confidence because Gildas himself does in a way provide us with a corrective to his highly prejudicial picture of Maelgwn. He tells us that this prince excelled all others in his physique, his generosity and in his ability to wage war. These facts should help us to disabuse our minds of any idea that Maelgwn was another Nero with a predilection for the company of obsequious poets, and to see that the bards in his court were, like those of later times, learned men entrusted with the custody of literary, historical and genealogical lore and charged with upholding the fame and dignity of their prince. This was a function of paramount importance, since allegiance to the chieftain and his family was almost the sole bond maintaining the unity of the tribe.

It is just possible that Maelgwn's bards knew and used to great effect an item of genealogical lore which has been preserved for us. It may not be historically true, and recently reasons for rejecting it have been advanced, but in Welsh tradition Maelgwn's great-grandfather was Cunedda, a chieftain who came to Wales from the region of Manaw Gododdin, the district round Clackmannan in southern Scotland, one hundred and forty-six years before Maelgwn reigned.

This information is found in a Latin work called *Historia Brittonum*. It was written, according to some scholars, about 800 A.D. and so it is one of our primary sources for the history of Wales between the time of Gildas in the sixth century and that of Geoffrey of Monmouth in the twelfth. Its author, or rather its compiler, was, it is believed, a Welshman whose name was latinised as Nennius or Nemniuus. He is said to have been a disciple of Elfoddw, who was a bishop, and, according to one tradition, the chief bishop in Gwynedd before he died in 809. It is certain that if Nennius had not known that Maelgwn's ancestor, Cunedda, had come from Manaw Gododdin, his teacher, Elfoddw, would have told him, for such an important fact would not have escaped the knowledge of such a prominent churchman, misleading though his title ' bishop ' may be.

Nennius was, however, conversant with the traditions of British courts other than that of Gwynedd, as his *Historia Brittonum* shows. Indeed, almost his only claim to scholarship rests on the fact that he brought together these traditions and all other historical materials on which he could lay his hands. His method is best described in his own words : " I have made a heap of all I have found !"

He used documents as well as oral traditions, and among the former there must have been a list of names of Northumbrian kings, the men who had led the invasion and conquest of great tracts of British territory between the Humber and the Forth, all along the east coast and far inland as well, during the second half of the sixth century. One of the most important of these kings was Ida, the founder of the Northumbrian royal line. He is said to have ruled between 547 and 559. After Nennius had copied his name from the list, he added some extremely valuable notes from British or Welsh traditions. First of all he writes :

"Then Eudeyrn (MS. *Dutigern*) at that time used to fight bravely against the nations of Angles."
Unfortunately, of this British king nothing more is known.

Next comes a sentence which is of vital importance to all students of early Welsh literature.

"Then Talhaearn Tad Awen (MS. *Talhaern Tataguen*) gained renown in poetry and Neirin and Taliessin and Bluchbard and Cian who is called Gueinth Guaut, gained renown together at the same time in British poetry."

The first question which arises in considering this paragraph is : what is meant by British poetry ? It obviously means poetry written by Britons wherever they were, and, as we shall see presently, the Britons were still in possession of southern Scotland, north-west and south-west England, as well as a much more extensive Wales than the present. It also means poetry in the British language. If we regard this British tongue as composed of several dialects, then one of these was an early form of Welsh. If we regard it as one language and ignore its dialects, Welsh remains as good a name as any for it. It is certain that Welsh is its only modern representative in these islands.

When we consider the poets named we find that Talhaearn, the Father of the Muse or of Inspiration, is mentioned on his own. Nennius obviously regarded him as a poet who flourished in Eudeyrn's time, that is, at the time the Britons were fighting against Ida. If this particular synchronism is correct, then Talhaearn must be assigned a date somewhere around 550. In other words, he must have been practising his art about the same time as those bards in Maelgwn Gwynedd's court on whom Gildas poured such scorn. Indeed, Talhaearn may have been one of them, for nothing is said to connect him exclusively with Eudeyrn, and if Maelgwn was such a powerful prince among the Britons and if he was so well known for his generosity, as Gildas suggests, then in that case Talhaearn must have been very different from other members of his order if he did not visit the royal court of Gwynedd.

However, all this is conjecture. Everything that we know of Talhaearn is found in this one sentence of Nennius's, and in the same way we have no other source of information concerning Bluchbard and Cian, though the latter must have been a famous poet in his time if *Gueinth Guaut* is a scribal error for *Guenith Guaut*, ' the wheat of song.'

Fortunately we know much more of the other two bards mentioned, namely Taliesin and Aneirin. Indeed, two manuscripts are extant which claim to give us the work of these two poets.

The manuscript called the Book of Taliesin was written *circa* 1275 or perhaps later. It contains many poems which cannot have been composed before the ninth and the tenth centuries, but among the poems which are attributed to Taliesin there are about twelve which show all the signs of being authentic, in particular those to Urien, Lord of Rheged, and his son Owain, to Gwallawg ap Lleennawg and Cynan ap Brochfael. The first of these persons, Urien, is mentioned by Nennius. He is said to have fought against two English kings,

Theodrick and Hussa. (Against the latter he had as allies Rhydderch Hen, Gwallawg and Morgant. One of these, Morgant, had Urien murdered, out of jealousy, it appears, for his skill in warfare).

These historical references, detailed as they are and in some cases supported by other sources, establish Urien as a ruler among the northern Britons in the second half of the sixth century. His territory, Rheged, cannot be precisely defined but it seems to have included parts of the present Galloway as well as Cumberland.

The poems addressed to him and to others by Taliesin are for the most part stylized official tributes. They describe in conventional terms the splendour of the prince's establishment, his hospitality and generosity to the poet, and, incidentally, they give us an idea of the sort of praise which the bards lavished on Maelgwn Gwynedd. The British or Welsh bard is obviously performing a duty similar to that discharged by bards among the continental Celts and in other heroic age communities in the Indo-European tradition. He might well have used the words of the Jewish court-poet : " My tongue is the pen of a ready writer. I recite the things I have made upon the king."

The manuscript of the Book of Aneirin was written about 1250, but Sir Ifor Williams, to whose researches we owe all or almost all our knowledge of early Welsh literature, has shown that there was in existence in the ninth century a written copy of at least one-fifth of the poem which it contains. The text as it stands begins with the words : ' Hwn yw e gododin. Aneirin ae cant.' ' This is the Gododdin. Aneirin sang it.' The word Gododdin has occurred already in the name of the district from which Maelgwn's ancestor, Cunedda, is said to have come to north Wales, that is, Manaw Gododdin. It is the name of the people known to Ptolemy in the second century as Ouotadinoi.

The occasion for the composition of the Gododdin poem was a disastrous expedition made about the year 600 by the warband of Mynyddawg Mwynfawr, Lord of Din Eiddyn or Ysgor Eiddyn, in the locality of the modern Edinburgh. This had as its objective the recapture of the strategically important Catraeth, Richmond or Catterick. The warband, three hundred in number, all experienced fighters, were feasted, it appears, for a year before they were sent on their fatal mission, and they proved their worth on the field of battle. They fought skilfully and bravely, but their valour was of no avail against the overwhelming numerical superiority of the enemy, and so they fought to the bitter end.

Aneirin does not describe the battle ; indeed, he has no central theme to develop. He is content to extol the members of that famous warband, and as he commemorates them he fastens on one or two of the distinguishing features in the character of each. One used to be breathless before a maiden although he was well worth his salt as a soldier. Another would rather leave his body on the field of battle than go to a wedding ! The whole poem is aptly described as a collection of elegies.

Aneirin's poem attracted to itself stray verses from the work of other poets. Thus there are two versions of one stanza from a poem celebrating the victory of the Britons of Strathclyde and the death of Domhnall Brecc, the king of the Irish kingdom of Dálriada, in west Scotland, at the battle of Strathcarron in the year 642. These versions are important because they show that the British bards of Strathclyde practised in the middle of the seventh century the same poetic art as that of the bards of the Gododdin.

That the bards of Wales had the same literary tradition as that of the northern Britons is proved by two poems which have survived in very late copies : one, an eulogy of Cadwallon ap Cadfan, the Welsh prince who defeated and slew Edwin of Northumbria in 632, may be by the bard Afan Ferddig ; the other, an elegy to Cynddylan ap Cyndrwyn, perhaps the work of Meigant, seems to contain references to some successful raid on a district in the vicinity of Lichfield.

Cadwallon's death near Hexham at the end of 633 put an end to any hopes which the Britons of Wales may have had of reversing whatever effects the battle of Chester (in 613 or 616) may have had on the link by land between them and their northern compatriots. And as their connexion with the Britons of the south-west had been severed as far back as 577 at the battle of Deorham, the Welsh were henceforth almost completely isolated. However, there was no reprieve for them from the necessity of fighting their old enemy.

Round about the middle of the ninth century the kingdom of Powys was hard pressed by the English. Its struggle is reflected in the work of a bard or a school of bards who composed a series of dramatic stories. These seem to be based on the conviction that the disasters suffered are the work of an implacable Fate which sees to it that Pride is brought low. They are woven round the sixth-century figure of Llywarch Hen and his sons, round his cousin Urien Rheged, and round the seventh-century figure Cynddylan and his sister Heledd, but actually they deal with the events or rather with the emotions aroused by the events enacted on the borders of Powys.

To give one example, Llywarch Hen urges his son, Gwên, to go to battle against the English invaders of Powys. Gwên goes, and, like his brothers before him, he is killed on the dyke. Then comes a magnificent elegy in which the father mourns the last and the best of his twenty-four sons.

Only the poetry in which the monologues and dialogues are cast has survived : the prose in which the narrative must have been couched has disappeared altogether. Incidentally, this particular use of prose and poetry resembles that of the epic found in early Sanskrit sources, and it suggests a tradition which goes back to Indo-European times.

The Llywarch Hen literature reminds us that the bards must have been story-tellers and saga-reciters at this time as well as in later ages, and the question arises, have we any examples of their work ?

On this point as on all other points discussed here, Sir Ifor Williams's researches have been most illuminating. He has shown that Nennius used a story concerning Vortigern or Gwrtheyrn as well as a life of St. Germanus to form sections 31 to 38 of his *Historia Brittonum*, and that this story can be regarded as one of the prototypes of the Four Branches of the *Mabinogi* and all other Welsh tales.

Sir Ifor has also traced back to an early period the first version of the prose and verse story which grew up around a legendary Taliesin who seems to have been confused with the equally legendary Myrddin Wyllt and to have vied with him in fame as a seer.

Both these legendary figures have fictitious poems to their credit, and they remind us that the bards or at least some of them had pretensions to visionary powers and to the ability to foretell events.

The best known of all Early Welsh vaticinal or prophetic poems, *Armes Prydein*, was composed about 930 A.D. It would be very gratifying to refer to it as the classic example of the work of a professional bard in the prophetic vein, but it is, in all probability, the work of a monk!

It seems that all clerics did not share Gildas's prejudice against the bards, and recent research shows that in Wales as in Ireland some of them proved themselves apt students of the bardic arts. Indeed, as the inheritors of the written Christian-classical culture, they may have played a far greater part than we think in the preservation of what remains of early Welsh literature.

THE WELSH DYNASTIES IN THE DARK AGES

Nora K. Chadwick

THE language which we now call Welsh was once spoken over the whole of southern Scotland, western England and Wales. In the fifth and sixth centuries it was already being introduced into Brittany by the early colonists from Wales and Cornwall. A traveller could have set off from Edinburgh, and walked through Cumberland, and south along the Welsh border to Land's End, and he would have had no difficulty in ordering his meals in Welsh all the way. He would have felt at home everywhere. The Romans had gone, and with them foreign domination, and centralised organisation. In the brief interval before the foundation of the Saxon kingdoms, independent Welsh-speaking chieftains — or to be exact British-speaking chieftains — were ruling everywhere in Britain south of the Scottish highlands.

Britain emerges as a number of individual kingdoms, each under its own native ruler. We know the names of many of them in the west because in the sixth century our earliest learned writer Gildas addressed what he was pleased to call a ' Little Admonition ' to five of the princes, all of whom he regards as sinners in high places. It is, in fact, a thundering denunciation ; but in the course of it he has left us our first portrait gallery of British rulers, albeit a highly prejudiced one. Elsewhere in his thesis he gives a historical sketch of earlier British history, leading up to the Saxon invasion in the fifth century, which he ascribes to a certain *superbus tyrannus*, a ' proud tyrant', whom later historians call Vortigern. The ' tyrant's ' kingdom is located in central and eastern Wales, in the first half of the fifth century ; but his power may in fact have extended much farther into eastern England, for he earned Gildas's relentless censure and an unenviable fame for

50

having invited the Saxons into Britain to help protect it against the Picts and other raiders from the north. In fact, however, Gildas himself tells us that in this matter he acted together with all his councillors (*omnes conciliarii*), and the Saxons seem to have been invited in as *foederati* according to the normal Roman custom. Among Gildas's own contemporaries in the sixth century the most famous is the great Maelgwn Gwynedd, whom he addresses as the ' Island Dragon', and whom he denounces as a powerful and ruthless conqueror, one whom, though superior to all the kings of Britain in his splendid and imposing person, and his early promise, has renounced the vows which he had taken as a holy monk and has closed his ears to heavenly music to give ear to his own minstrels pouring forth songs of praise to himself and his retinue at the court feasts.

This is the period which we may call the British or Welsh heroic age, when the Britons of the north put up a valiant resistance to the Saxon invasions. But the British territory was not easily defensible, for it stretched from south-eastern Scotland to Cornwall in a long strip with a double frontier, east and west. So long as the Romans had been to the east and south the Britons could defend their northern and western frontiers with confidence, containing the Picts behind the Highland Line, and confining the Irish encroachments to the outer peninsulas. But with the departure of the Romans, and the Saxon advances from the east, the Britons had to face about and encounter a new enemy where their former friends had been, leaving their rear unprotected against the Irish. And the Irish menace was a very real one. Like the Saxons in the east, the Irish were forming settlements all the way up the west coast from Cornwall to Argyll.

It was to expel the Irish from the western sea-board that a certain Cunedda is said to have come to Wales from south-eastern Scotland, some time in the fifth century, and with him came eight of his sons ; and we are told that " they expelled the Irish from all British districts." Cunedda is perhaps the most important figure in early Welsh tradition, for a number of the genealogies of the north Welsh princes trace their ancestry back to his sons, who are represented as founders of early Welsh kingdoms. If we can trust the story, Cunedda founded a dynasty which shaped the future of Wales.

Not all the Welsh kingdoms claimed to be descended from Cunedda. Some of the other kingdoms have very different origins, especially in the east and south. Pembroke, or Dyfed as the earlier and wider kingdom of Pembroke was called, claimed with good reason to have been of Irish origin. The little mountain kingdom of Brycheiniog (or Brecknock) is another which was never at any time subject to Cunedda's sons, and its rulers claimed to be descended from a native princess and an Irish prince from Pembroke or even Ireland itself. Perhaps that is why Brycheiniog possesses the only Welsh *crannog*, or lake dwelling of Irish type, in Llan-gors lake, and shares with Pembrokeshire and Carmarthenshire the distinction of having more inscriptions in the Irish alphabet called *ogham* — seven in all — than any other Welsh area. Powys also had a native dynasty independent of Cunedda's ' sons ' — beautiful and fertile Powys, which the author of the ' Llywarch Hen ' poems calls the ' paradise of Wales'. This kingdom seems to have had an unbroken development since Roman times, and still earlier from the British kingdom of the Cornovii, with Wroxeter as its tribal centre and the Wrekin as its watch-tower. Powys was the gateway into Wales from England, and the most vulnerable point — always a battle-ground. It had to be constantly on the defensive.

These and other genealogies of the earliest Welsh royal families show Wales in the Dark Ages as a little chess-board of small kingdoms, each independent, and ruled by a dynasty inheriting from father to son. As we trace their separate histories till we draw towards the gradual unification of Wales in the ninth century, and finally to the close association with England in the tenth, we shall be surprised at the length of time during which these kingdoms lasted and remained intact. Some of their ruling families had a life of more than 500 years. Their long continuity implies a peaceful and civilised country, free from serious internal wars, free from external aggression.

The sixth century, the century which followed the establishment of the Welsh kingdoms, is known in Wales, as in other Celtic lands, as the age of the saints. Following on the heroic

age of the Celtic revival after the departure of the Romans came
a period of peaceful intellectual and spiritual development and
of political expansion overseas to Brittany. Throughout the
whole of south Wales, and even central Wales and Ceredigion,
the princes themselves and the monks of the early Celtic
Church, who generally belonged to the same families, established churches and centres of education in Wales, and founded
in Brittany our earliest colony. The introduction and rapid
spread of the art of writing gave a prestige to ecclesiastics which
made them indispensable to the hereditary princes, and substituted diplomacy for the sword. Prince and ' saint ' jointly
founded Brittany by a peaceful penetration, and instituted a
two-way traffic overseas which gave to Wales a wider horizon,
and at the same time stimulated her intellectual development
by contact with the Gallo-Roman culture of Armorica or
Brittany. It was in Brittany that all our earliest Welsh saints'
' Lives ' were written.

In Wales itself the level of culture was relatively high, even
in these early times. The royal pedigrees were carefully preserved by a trained professional class. The laws were also
handed down by word of mouth from ancient times, as we can
see if we compare them with the Irish codes ; but they were
modified from time to time, and from one district to another
as the centuries went by, and even humorous touches found
their way in here and there, so that they sometimes make
rather amusing reading. Such is the penalty for killing or
stealing a cat which guards the king's barn :—

> ' Its head is to be held downward on a clean, level floor,
> and its tail is to be held upwards ; and after that wheat
> must be poured over it until the tip of its tail is hidden,'

and that is its value, to which some cat fancier has added a
note on the points of a well-bred cat :—

> ' It should be perfect of ear, perfect of eye, perfect of teeth,
> perfect of claw, without marks of fire, and it should kill mice,
> and not devour its kittens, and it should not go cater-wauling
> every new moon.'

But in fact these so-called Welsh ' laws ' contain much which
is really outside the strict definition of a legal code, and include
compendia of various kinds of information relating to such

matters as the different grades and relative prestige of the
military and civil officials ; the stipends and emoluments of
servants and members of the royal household, including poets
and harpers ; specifications of the wardrobes of court officers
and their perquisites ; as well as carefully graded penalties for
various classes of legal offences.

Poetry was popular with all classes, chanted, of course, not
written. Bards and professional story-tellers carried on the
traditions and the historical poetry, especially elegies, and
poems in praise of the great Welsh heroes of the past. The
people had a rich intellectual life, quite different from ours
to-day, with their ancient history stored in their memories, and
constantly brought to their minds by the bards at the feast in
the evening, when all were gathered together in the great hall.
These early poetical themes, and the history of early Powys,
have inspired much of the poetry attributed to Llywarch Hen ;
and the beautiful prose stories and myths of early Wales, which
we can still read in the *Mabinogion*, have lost nothing of their
grace and charm in their passage down the centuries from these
early days.

There was poetry for all classes and all ages. The sixth
century poet Taliesin has left us a vignette of Brochmael's
little heroic court on the Severn :—

" I sang," he tells us in a poem, " before a famous prince in
the meadows of the Severn, before Brochmael of Powys who
loved my *Awen* ", that is to say, " who valued my poetic inspiration and patronised my art." Gildas recalls boatmen singing sailors' songs beneath the swelling sails ; and Sir Ifor
Williams has interpreted for us an enchanting lullaby, probably
composed by a *bardd teulu*, or household bard. The mother
sings to her little child Dinogad :—

> ' When thy father went a-hunting
> With spear on shoulder, and cudgel in hand,
> He would call his big dogs,
> ' Giff, Gaff' ; ' Catch, Catch ' ; ' Fetch, Fetch' ;
> In his coracle he would spear a fish,
> Striking suddenly like a lion.
> When thy father went up the mountain
> He would bring back a roe-buck, a wild boar, a stag,

A spotted grouse from the mountains,
A fish from the falls of Derwennydd.
Of those which thy father reached with his spear
Not one would escape which was not winged."

Inscriptions in stone best illustrate the level of culture of these Welsh kingdoms from the fifth to the seventh centuries. It was the Romans who first taught the Britons to set up inscribed tombstones ; but the inscribed stones of Wales show clearly that the sea-routes from Gaul were open in the Dark Ages up the west coast, and new influences were coming in at this time. New names are now in fashion, Paulinus, Sadwrn (from *Saturnius*), Martin. An inscription in Caernarvonshire to *Melus medicus*, ' Melus the physician ', son of one Martin, shows that the professional doctor was now a man of science and not a magician. There is a famous stone in the church at Llangadwaladr in Anglesey to king Cadfan (who died *c.* 625), and it reads like a barbaric attempt at verse :—

Catamannus rex :
Sapientissimus, opinatissimus,
Omnium regum.

' King Cadfan, most learned and most renowned of all kings.' As the late Dr. Nash-Williams observed, it echoes the grandiloquent phraseology of the contemporary Byzantine court ; and the lettering is the very latest thing in Carolingian epigraphy. The court at Aberffraw on the Anglesey coast prided itself on its culture, and was rich enough to keep abreast of continental developments.

The stone, however, was probably erected to Cadfan's memory by his son Cadwallon, or his grandson Cadwaladr, the founder of the church. Cadwallon had fought to the death against the great Edwin of Northumbria for the *imperium* of all Britain — nothing less. The warfare of Gwynedd in the seventh century was waged on the grand scale, and for great issues. The stone to the memory of King Cadfan looks very much like the claim of a Welsh prince to be *Bretwalda*. Had not Cadwallon been slain in battle in an attack on Northumbria, the claim might indeed have been realised.

And all the time the English encroachments continue on the border. It was the royal line of Powys, the descendants of Brochmael Ysgythrwg, who bore the brunt of these attacks.

In 716 or 717 the Northumbrian king Aethelfrith, Edwin's
predecessor, made an attack on Chester in which the reigning
king of Powys, Selyf the son of Cynan Garwyn, and grandson
of Brochmael, was slain, and a great number of the monks of
the neighbouring monastery of Bangor-on-the-Dee were put
to the sword. It is the greatest border disaster on record, and
must have been widely renowned in elegy and saga, for it is
recorded independently in the Annals of Wales, also in two of
the earliest collections of Irish annals and even in the pages of
Bede. Late in the same century Offa's Dyke cut off a large
portion of the old kingdom of Powys — the richest portion; and
from the poems associated with the name of Llywarch Hen we
learn of the desolation wrought round Pengwern, or Shrewsbury, and in the hall of Cynddylan its lord —

> ' The court of Pengwern is a raging fire . . .
> The hall of Cynddylan is dark tonight,
> Without fire, without a bed.
> I weep a while, then fall silent.'

Yet neither the military power nor the high heart of Powys
was crushed. Her finest memorial is the pillar cross in the vale
of Llangollen, set up in the first half of the ninth century by
Concenn, or Cyngen, the last king of this dynasty, to com-
memorate a crushing defeat by his great-grandfather Elise, a
descendant of Brochmael, on the people beyond Offa's dyke.
" It is Elise," reads this proud record, graven in stone, "who
annexed the heritage of Powys . . . from the power of the
English, which he made into a sword-land by fire."

And Cyngen, who set up this fine war memorial, seems here
to claim once more the possession of all Powys. He died in
Rome in 854, the first Welsh king known to have visited the
Continent. The opening of a letter containing a greeting from
Merfyn to Concenn, and preserved in a MS. at Bamberg, is
probably the earliest Welsh letter in existence, and was doubt-
less addressed to him by his brother-in-law Merfyn, king of
Gwynedd.

We have reached the close of the first great period of Welsh
history, with its numerous small, independent kingdoms ; and
we have arrived at what the Rev. A. W. Wade-Evans has
rightly called the " emergence of Wales.' The second phase of
Welsh history now begins — the gradual absorption of most

of the Welsh ruling dynasties by the royal house of Gwynedd in the north, and the gradual approximation to a Wales united under a single family.   It is, I think, the most remarkable feature of early Welsh history that the union of most of these kingdoms should have come about gradually with no record of conquest and no bloodshed.   Those historians who speak of the Welsh as a warlike people see Wales only through the eyes of the Norman conquerors, when the whole country became an armed fortress on the defensive.   The early history is very different — a history of peaceful development, of gradual unification by policy, and by a series of royal marriages.

The ' unification ' began in the ninth century, when, as the late Sir John Lloyd put it, a stranger sat upon the throne of Gwynedd.   This new king, Merfyn Frych, traced his ancestry to the ' North ', as the Welsh called the princely families of the British of southern Scotland.   Merfyn may have belonged to a family settled in the Isle of Man, but his father had married into the ancient family of the great Maelgwn Gwynedd, and Merfyn seems to have inherited Gwynedd through his mother. Perhaps he was not wholly a stranger after all.

Merfyn knew that the gateway from England to Wales lay through Powys.   Forthwith he barred it by marrying Nest, the sister of Cyngen — that last king of the native dynasty of Powys who had set up the pillar of victory against the English.   The son of Merfyn and Nest was presumably the heir to both Gwynedd and Powys, and with them to the full weight of responsibility for the border defences.   This son was Rhodri Mawr.

Rhodri was the greatest of all the Welsh kings.   His ordeal was the most severe of any in early Welsh history, with the growing power of the Saxons in the east, and the new menace of the Vikings in the west.   No saga or life of Rhodri has come down to us, but his achievements speak for themselves.   By the middle of the ninth century he was the most powerful ruler in Wales, and the founder of its leading family.   In 856 he killed Gorm, the leader of the Viking fleet off Anglesey, and we gather from continental writings that he won the gratitude of the Frankish king, Charles the Bald, who was suffering even more severely at Viking hands.   Earliest of all Welsh kings Rhodri seems to have brought Wales into relations with foreign powers, and his court comes before us as a centre of native culture and foreign contacts. Here several languages could be heard — Welsh, Irish, perhaps one or two continental tongues, and also the Latin of the scholars, both insular and continental.

His home policy was no less significant. Like his father Merfyn, he added to his kingdom by a diplomatic marriage. His wife was Angharad, the sister of the last king of Cardigan. This was a master-stroke, for Cardigan had already been joined to Carmarthen and now formed the wide new kingdom of Seisyllwg, cutting off the Pembrokeshire peninsula. Rhodri, as a ruler of Seisyllwg, thus set a hedge of fire between Pembroke and the other southern kingdoms, all of them in panic at his growing power. It is interesting to speculate what Rhodri's next move would have been if he had not been killed in battle against the English in 878. Could he have checkmated the policy of his great contemporary, Alfred the Great, who was working for a pro-English party in south Wales ?

Rhodri's grandson, Hywel Dda, son of Rhodri's son Cadell, prince of Cardigan, now takes over the chess-board with two brilliant moves. First he put Pembroke out of her misery by marrying Elen, the daughter of her king, thus making their interests one, and turning an enemy into a friend. This eventually gave him all south-western Wales, known as Deheubarth. Then eventually on the death of Rhodri's grandson, Idwal, ruling in Gwynedd, he quietly annexed Gwynedd, and with it doubtless Powys also, and found himself ruler of practically all Wales. He had shifted the centre of power from north Wales to south.

This is the third and last phase of independent Wales. We are now on the eve of the close association with England. It was no sudden change. A party had been growing in the south which held the heroic patriotism of Rhodri and the north as out-of-date, and favoured a wider outlook and co-operation with Wessex. And no wonder, with the hostile English the other side of Offa's Dyke, and the Vikings surging round the shores. Yet south Wales was not a united party in this policy of co-operation with England, as we can see from the *Armes Prydein*. This, the last great patriotic poem of Wales, composed early in the tenth century, calls all the Celtic peoples and the

Norse of Dublin to unite and drive the hated Saxons back to their poverty-striken homes across the North Sea. Yet the dominant party in south Wales, no less than the West Saxons themselves, realised the danger of the Viking menace to their mutual safety, and it is significant that in the great struggle of 937 between Athelstan on the one hand, and a combined force of Scots, Danes, and the Britons of the north on the other, the south Welsh took no part. The rapprochement with England for which Alfred was already working in the ninth century was finally effected between Hywel Dda and Athelstan in the tenth.

The shift of political power from north to south under Hywel Dda, and the cultivation of friendship with Wessex, brought an inevitable change of outlook. The traditional standards and ideals inherited from the heroic age and the men of the north — love of independence, reckless courage, personal loyalty to the death — all these are now subordinated to an institutionalised society. The name of Hywel Dda stands at the head of the earliest written code of Welsh laws. The earliest coin struck by a Welsh king bears the legend *Hywel Rex*. Hywel was not only following the example of English kings by introducing English institutions into his own country. He was giving active co-operation to Athelstan by acting as a witness to his charters, many of which bear Hywel's signature.

During the Dark Ages the Welsh dynasties have been living through a struggle between two opposing ideals and two opposing forces — the heroic ideals and brilliant military achievements in the early history of the north ; and the later realism and political sagacity of the south. We have stepped out of the old world into the new. Rhodri is undoubtedly the greatest and the most imposing figure in early Welsh history. To Rhodri we owe the growth and union of the Welsh nation ; the loss of Welsh separatism we owe to his grandson Hywel Dda, who sacrificed it to a constructive co-operation with his nearest and most powerful neighbours. By closer relations with Wessex he made Wales a partaker in the profits gained in the course of centuries of advancing civilisation from the great European countries. Call it opportunism if you will ; but it was the union of Celt with Saxon which helped to save Britain from a foreign domination.

THE AGE OF THE SAINTS

By Emrys G. Bowen

WE know that there were a few Christians in Wales during the period of the Roman occupation, but the only archæological evidence for their existence is to be found in south-eastern Wales, where the Roman occupation was most marked. After the withdrawal of the Roman forces, Christianity was re-introduced into Wales from Gaul by way of the western sea-routes, and the Celtic Church seems to have arisen from the fusion of this Gallo-Roman Christianity of imperial days in the south-eastern borderland. Anyway, between the fifth and the eighth centuries A.D. the whole of the country was christianized by the wandering monks and missionaries of the Celtic Church, who were later called ' saints ' — although, of course, not one of them was officially canonised by the Church of Rome. The saints left a permanent impression on the countryside, not only by their zeal and enthusiasm but also by their methods of evangelisation.

Inspired by the new movement, members of royal households and others adopted the religious life, the more famous attracting to themselves many disciples. In this way grew up such institutions as that of Llantwit Major (Llanilltud Fawr) where St. Illtud taught, and Llancarfan (also in the Vale of Glamorgan) where St. Cadoc had his famous school. In turn, individual monks accompanied by a few followers would set out from one of the great monastic schools on what we would now call a missionary journey. The saint in question might halt at a chosen spot, and set up a simple cross and preach to the people. If the mission was successful a tiny church would be built, made of wattle and daub, and at the same time a few cells would be erected to house the little company. The settlement would probably be enclosed by earthen ramparts as a protection against man and beast. Such settlements were

known in ancient Wales by the word ' llan ' — a word that was
used in later times for the church alone.   The little churches
that grew up on these sites frequently carried the name of the
saint who first established them.   Should the settlement be well
placed a small village or hamlet would, in due course, gather
around it, so that such places as Llandeilo, Llanbadarn and
Llanbedrog are the successors of the original settlements established on these sites by St. Teilo, St. Padarn and St. Petroc
respectively.   Towards the close of their lives, and in some
cases very much earlier, the wandering saints would feel the
urge ' to seek the desert'.   They would seek a lonely place
(possibly a hill-top, a promontory, or an island off the shore)
whereon to build a tiny cell and there to live henceforth the life
of a hermit.   In later times the tradition that a holy man once
dwelt on the site would be sufficient to attract pilgrims, and
soon a little church bearing his name would be erected on the
spot.   In this way the Welsh countryside, in common with
that of other Celtic countries, is dotted with memorials of the
age of the saints.

The importance of this period in the history of Wales is,
therefore, clear ; the difficulties consist of attempting a
scientific history of this age.   The first problem concerns the
literary sources.   There are many ' Lives ' of the saints which
purport to be the history of individual saints, describing in
great detail their reputed ancestry, their travels and the miracles
they wrought.   The trouble is, however, that with very rare
exceptions these ' Lives ' were written up some six hundred
years or more after the saint in question is supposed to have
lived, and at a time when all real information concerning him
or her had long since been forgotten.   The result is that the
' Lives ' themselves are constructed on a somewhat standardised
pattern and are packed full of stories recording the remarkable
miracles of the saint and acts of divine interference, which are
of little significance to the modern historian.   Unfortunately,
too, the original settlements established by the saints were, as
I have said, most frequently built of soft earth and timber, and
little, therefore, remains for the modern archæologist to discover.   In brief, both the literary and archæological sources
relative to the age of the saints are, for one reason or another,

unsatisfactory. Modern work, therefore, is turning to the topographical evidence.

From what has already been said it is a relatively simple matter to plot on a map all the known ancient dedications to, say, St. Teilo, St. Cadoc or St. Illtud, and in this way obtain what is called the *patria*, or the sphere of influence, of a particular saint. In recent years I have prepared such maps for all the known Celtic saints in Wales, and the study of the geographical distributions of these dedications is most revealing, shedding new light on this obscure period. The most significant thing that emerges is that these distribution patterns are in no way haphazard, but clearly reflect distribution patterns resulting from the plotting of prehistoric settlements or finds. It follows, therefore, that the various areas in which individual saints operated were, at that remote time, already long-established culture areas. This evidence alone brings the work of the saints within the accepted framework of our present knowledge of the history of Britain in both the pre-Roman and the post-Roman centuries.

Before describing some of the more important distributions a word of caution is once more necessary. We know that it is not only likely but in some cases certain, that churches were dedicated to Celtic saints at a time very much later than the fifth to the eighth centuries A.D. If there were a very large number of such dedications, then the validity of arguing from the distributions back to the age of the saints would be considerably weakened. Actually, however, it can be shown that when medieval dedications took place they invariably fell within the original *patria* of the saint in question.

We can now proceed with the main argument. The dedication distribution patterns fall into three clearly marked groups; one is based on south-eastern Wales and the neighbouring borderland, a second concerns south-west Wales, and a third embraces north Wales. By attempting to arrange the three patterns in their chronological order we can reconstruct in some measure a new outline history of the age of the saints in Wales.

As I have said, everything points to the fact that the earliest evidence of the Celtic saints is to be found in south-eastern Wales. Not only was there some Christianity in these parts in imperial times, but also, following upon the Saxon invasions, many refugees from the important Christian communities around Silchester and Cirencester spread westward into the Hereford–Monmouth hills. On the other hand, the late Dr. Nash-Williams has produced abundant evidence in his great work, *The Early Christian Monuments of Wales*, to show that many Christians, hailing ultimately from the Lyon and Vienne areas of Gaul, landed on the western peninsulas of Wales. Judging by the distribution of their tombstones, many of these Gallo-Roman immigrants moved eastwards across the country following what remained of the former Roman roads. In this way they were led naturally into south-eastern Wales where they met the Christians we have already described. The Gaulish immigrants may well have introduced the eremitical form of Christianity which came ultimately from the early Christian Fathers in the Egyptian desert and was reinforced in the west by the example of St. Martin of Tours. Anyway, we find this eremitical idea strongly represented in Celtic Christianity combined with other elements that might have been derived from the Christianity of Roman Britain. It is in precisely such a context that we hear of St. Dubricius, the bulk of whose churches are to be found in the Hereford–Monmouth borderland. Tradition connects him closely with St. Germanus, the famous bishop of Auxerre, who was certainly in Britain, and involved in the politico-religious history of this borderland, in the mid-fifth century.

The cult of St. Dubricius spread away from the south-eastern borderland along the Roman roads to Gwenddwr in Breconshire and southwards, by sea, to Porlock on the north coast of Somerset. Everything seems to point, therefore, to St. Dubricius being one of the earliest of the Celtic saints. Such a view is strongly suggested by the surviving topographical evidence. At a slightly later date, saints like Cadoc and Illtud, whom we have already mentioned, emerged in this area. The majority of the ancient churches bearing their names are located in south-eastern Wales although their cults, too, spread westwards and south-westwards both by land and sea.

Many of the later stories we possess concerning these men seem to echo the semi-Roman atmosphere in which they lived.

Cadoc is said to have been descended from the emperor Augustus and to have loved the pagan poets, especially Virgil, while stories of St. Illtud bring out, even more clearly, the overlapping cultures characteristic of the south-eastern borderland at this time. For example, we have an interesting reference to St. Illtud in the *Life* of St. Samson of Dol. This *Life* is one of the exceptions to the general rule concerning their late authorship. It is known to be of very early date — possibly a generation or so after the events it describes. In this way its statements deserve close attention. It describes St. Samson being taken as a youth to Illtud's great school at Llanilltud Fawr. This is what is said of Illtud. " Now this Eltud was the most learned of all the Britons in his knowledge of the Scriptures, both the Old Testament and the New Testament, and in every branch of philosophy, poetry and rhetoric, grammar and arithmetic, and he was most sagacious and gifted with the power of foretelling future events." This could, with justification, be taken to mean that one-third of the saint's background was that of a Christian teacher, another third that of an educated Roman gentleman, and the remaining third that of a pagan soothsayer, or, possibly, a Druid. These, indeed, may represent the various culture elements present in south-eastern Wales in the immediate post-Roman centuries, and be a very accurate picture of what St. Illtud was really like.

It is now time to turn to the saints of south-west Wales. Here the most famous names are those of David (Dewi, the patron saint) and Teilo. There is considerable topographical evidence to suggest that these men worked together, as the churches bearing their names frequently occur in the same areas. All the traditions concerning Dewi are linked with Cardiganshire and Pembrokeshire culminating, of course, in his famous settlement at Tyddewi. The headquarters of St. Teilo's cult was at Llandeilo Fawr in Carmarthenshire. Both seem to have been great preachers and evangelists rather than great scholars, as we think Saints Cadoc and Illtud might have been. The south-western saints relied on the spoken word. Think of the famous story of St. David addressing the synod at Llanddewibrefi with the ground rising miraculously under his feet so that he had a better pulpit. David was praised for his asceticism and hard work. To many he was known as Dewi Ddyfrwr — David the Waterman.

So great was the evangelical fervour of these men that they would appear to have encompassed the older forms of the faith in the south-east. Dewi and Teilo between them have many churches in Radnorshire and Breconshire and David is represented even in western Herefordshire. We find their cults, too, spreading into the south-east by way of southern Carmarthenshire and the coastal zone of Glamorgan. The presence of large numbers of Dewi and Teilo churches in the south-eastern province presented a real problem to the Norman bishops attempting to organise the dioceses of Llandaff and St. David's on a territorial basis in early Middle Ages. The well-known *Llyfr Llandaf* (The Book of Llandaff) is an attempt to present the claims of the south-eastern diocese.

The remaining province for consideration is the domain of the men of the north. Fundamental cultural distinctions between north and south Wales reach back deeply into prehistoric times. The south has always derived its culture from south-eastern Britain, or from the sea, while the north has looked more to Yorkshire, Northumberland and southern Scotland. It was likewise in the age of the saints. We know that Gaulish Christianity reached Whithorn in south-western Scotland by way of the western sea-routes at the same time as Gaulish Christian refugees reached Wales, and that there was some form of Christianity in the southern uplands of Scotland before the mission of St. Columba, based on Iona. With the Roman withdrawal, folk movements ensued between the men of the north and their kinsmen in north Wales — movements which became crystallised in the story of the sons of Cunedda. Many of the saints of north Wales, such as those traditionally described as descended from Cunedda or Coel Godebog were, undoubtedly, among the camp followers of these great movements. The remarkable thing, however, is that, among the whole list of north Wales saints known to us, there are very few outstanding names — few, indeed, that can compare with the great names found in the south-east and south-west. More remarkable still is the fact that the greatest name of all in the north, judged by the number of ancient dedications bearing his

name — St. Beuno — would appear to be more closely linked
culturally with the south than with the north, although he has
but one dedication in the south, and that, strictly, not in Wales
at all. Llanfeuno-under-Clodock is an ancient dedication to
St. Beuno, set among a cluster of Dewi churches in south-
western Herefordshire. As late as the eleventh century there is
well attested archæological evidence linking this area with the
St. David's district in Pembrokeshire, showing that contact
between the areas continued long after the days of Dewi and
Beuno. Could it, therefore, be that (as tradition asserts) St.
Beuno received his education in these parts and that it was an
education in the evangelical Davidic tradition ? In due course,
he carried the Dewi asceticism into both Powys and Gwynedd.
What Tyddewi and Llandeilo Fawr are to the south, Clynnog
Fawr is to the north. Whatever our views may be on the
matter, it is at least curious that a fourteenth century anchorite
in one of Dewi's most famous cells (Llanddewibrefi in Cardiganshire) should have thought it appropriate to re-write the life-
story of this otherwise exclusively northern Saint in the same
book as he re-wrote the *Life* of St. David. In this way, although
there is not a single ancient dedication to St. David in the whole
of north Wales, his influence in these parts, through the mission
of St. Beuno, might have been great indeed.

There can be no doubt that the age of the saints is a formative
period in Welsh history. It was they who first created a
Christian Wales. Hundreds of churches, scattered throughout
the land, still bear their names; while the sites they established
and the settlements that developed upon them bear witness to
the basic contributions they made to the Wales we know today.

THE LAWS OF HYWEL DDA

By J. Goronwy Edwards

IF any of the old Welsh preachers of my boyhood had been faced with this sort of topic, they would probably have begun by observing that the subject is one which ' divides itself naturally under two headings', firstly, ' The Laws ', and secondly, ' Hywel Dda '. That division happens to be very convenient for our present purpose, so I am going to adopt it : I shall try to deal with precisely those two points, and I shall take them in just that order, because for the historian that is their true order of importance : firstly, ' The Laws ' ; secondly (and secondarily), ' Hywel Dda '.

Firstly, ' The Laws '. By ' The Laws ' we mean, in this case, the Welsh laws which governed Wales in the Middle Ages, but which eventually — say by about the middle of the sixteenth century — were superseded by English law. Now the laws of a people are very important for the historian because on the one hand they reflect that people's way of life, and because on the other hand they also shape it ; of that way of life, the laws are at once a mirror and a mould. The Welsh laws current in Wales during the Middle Ages have precisely that twofold importance for the Welsh historian. If there were time, that statement could easily be illustrated by examples, but I need not stop to do so now, because later speakers will be providing you with some illustrations. Instead, let us consider another and rather different aspect of the subject. How do we know about these Welsh laws ? How do we know their content — how do we know what rules of conduct they prescribed for the men and women who lived under them ?

Our main source of information about the content of Welsh law is a series of some seventy manuscripts lawbooks which survive, most of them in Welsh but a few in Latin, in various great libraries.

About half of these seventy manuscripts are late copies made during the sixteenth, seventeenth and eighteenth centuries : these copies were made by or for various scholars of the sixteenth, seventeenth and eighteenth centuries who were interested in Welsh antiquities ; by that time the Welsh laws had become antiquities, for they were no longer actually current in Wales as a live legal system.

The other half of the seventy surviving manuscripts, however, were written before the sixteenth century — say between 1200 or a little earlier, and 1500 or a little later — in other words, these manuscripts belong to the period before the Welsh laws had been superseded in Wales, to the period when the Welsh laws were a live system in Wales : they were written, not for scholarly antiquarians, but for practising lawyers. For that reason, it is these medieval copies of the Welsh lawbooks that really matter to the historian. As I have already indicated, there are some thirty-five of them still surviving, and there were probably at one time or another a good many more copies which are no longer in existence. It is worth noticing, by the way, that the number of Welsh lawbooks of medieval date still surviving — some thirty-five — is much the same as the numbers of surviving manuscripts of the two most important books of medieval English law, I mean the books known respectively as Glanvill and Bracton : of Glanvill there are some twenty-seven surviving manuscripts ; of Bracton there are some forty-six.

How were our medieval Welsh lawbooks compiled ? Fortunately one of them has told us. In its preface, it says that its author, named Iorwerth ap Madog, had put it together from four other books, which are named, ' and also along with these', the preface continues, ' from the best books which he found in Gwynedd, and Powys, and Deheubarth'. In other words, this particular lawbook specifically describes itself as a compilation derived (at any rate very largely) from previously existing lawbooks. And indeed we can draw that conclusion for ourselves, even without the specific statement of the preface, by just comparing the text of Iorwerth's book with the corresponding parts of the other Welsh lawbooks. In fact, all the medieval Welsh lawbooks were compilations of the same kind, and that is proved by two considerations : on the one hand, all the Welsh lawbooks have a great deal of matter in common ; and on the other hand, they show many traces of having been patched together from a variety of sources. This patchwork character of the Welsh lawbooks is one of their most interesting and valuable features from the historian's point of view.

When, however, we compare the contents of the various Welsh lawbooks it soon becomes evident that their compilers were apt to do a good deal more than merely reproduce existing lawbooks. A compiler not infrequently tacked additional matter on to the pre-existing text which he was using. For instance, if legal opinion had come to be divided on some principle enunciated in his pre-existing text, the compiler of the new version would often add a note at the appropriate point stating what the alternative legal opinion was, and indicating the reasons for it. Or again, there are a number of instances in which a compiler has supplemented his pre-existing text by introducing short treatises on such matters as the procedure, or the forms of pleading, used in the courts for various types of cases. Or again, one compiler has introduced what he calls ' a Book of the Rudiments of the Law of Hywel Dda,' in other words, the A B C of Hywel's law, while another has brought in what is in effect a sort of legal catechism in the form of a series of questions and answers on a number of legal matters. This catechism and the Book of Rudiments were evidently intended for the use of those who were teaching and learning Welsh law : there are, incidentally, other indications in the lawbooks that medieval Welsh lawyers did undergo some course of instruction, though we know very little about its form.

What I have said will be sufficient, I hope, to indicate the nature of our medieval Welsh lawbooks. They have often been referred to as ' codes ' of Welsh law. But the term ' code ' does not really apply to them. A legal code, in the proper sense of the term, should provide a statement of the law which is both reasonably complete — at any rate at the time when it was drawn up — and is also systematically arranged. The Welsh lawbooks are neither sufficiently complete nor sufficiently systematic to deserve to be called ' codes.' Yet they do in one way and another record the substance of a great deal of the

Welsh law that was current in medieval Wales, and they do make some attempt at arranging that law under headings. On the whole, perhaps the best way of describing the medieval Welsh lawbook, as we know it, would be to say that it was a lawyer's compendium, that it was a book which might have been given some such title as ' The Legal Practitioner's Companion to Welsh Law.' So much for my first point — ' The Laws ' — and the lawbooks in which they are recorded. As I have said, those lawbooks contain perfectly sound statements about a very considerable body of medieval Welsh law. But they also contain something else. They also contain a certain amount of what purports to be medieval Welsh history. And their statements about Welsh history are by no means as sound as many of their statements about Welsh law. That brings me to my second heading — ' Hywel Dda '.

Hywel was not known as ' Hywel Dda ' during his lifetime : the epithet ' Da,' ' the Good ', was not applied to him until later. His proper name was Hywel ap Cadell. He was a Welsh king who ruled from about 910 A.D. until his death about 950 A.D. For the greater part of his time he was king only in Deheubarth, i.e. in south-west Wales, but in his last years he extended his authority over Gwynedd and quite possibly over Powys as well, i.e. over north Wales and mid-Wales. These facts may be regarded as historically certain, because they are vouched for by (among other sources) the Welsh chronicle which is contemporaneous with Hywel. But Hywel is famous in Welsh history as the great lawgiver of medieval Wales. Now his fame as a lawgiver rests upon a tradition which goes back quite a long way, but we have no certainty that it is a tradition which goes as far back as Hywel's own time. The tradition as we have it is first recorded in the Welsh lawbooks of which I have already spoken. The earliest surviving copies of those lawbooks, you will remember, come from about 1200 A.D. So the tradition that Hywel was a great lawgiver is not recorded until the close of the twelfth century, i.e. more than two centuries later than Hywel's own time. Of course the tradition may quite well have existed earlier than the first surviving Welsh lawbooks in which we find it first recorded, but if so, we do not at present know how much earlier it did exist, and therefore we cannot at present say with any certainty how and when the tradition began. What then is the tradition recorded by the Welsh lawbooks about Hywel as a lawgiver, and in what form do they record it ?

All the surviving Welsh lawbooks, except those which have accidentally lost their opening pages, begin with a sort of preface, and it is in that preface that they tell us what they have to say about Hywel as a lawgiver. The essential points of their story are four :

(1) That Hywel summoned an assembly consisting of the chief ecclesiastics of Wales, together with six men from each of the local sub-divisions of the country ;

(2) That this assembly examined and discussed the laws of Wales for a period of forty days ;

(3) That as a result of their deliberations they made various changes and improvements in the laws ; and

(4) That the laws as thus revised were set down in writing and embodied in an authoritative book.

On those four main points all the prefaces are in agreement. But some of the prefaces supply more details than others. For instance, while some of the prefaces make no more than the bare statement that the revised laws were written in a book, other prefaces go on to say that the revised law was put into written form by thirteen of the wisest members of the assembly, headed by a very learned man whose name is given as Master Blegywryd ; while other prefaces again go still further, stating that Master Blegywryd was archdeacon of Llandaff, and that he held the degree of Doctor of Laws. When we examine this and all the other pieces of additional information more closely, one very significant fact comes out pretty clearly ; we find that the more numerous the details which a preface contains, the later in date is the manuscript to which that preface belongs. Now the presence in these prefaces of these successive layers of additional details becoming more and more numerous as the lawbooks get later and later in date, is a phenomenon which is perfectly familiar to historians in documents other than the Welsh lawbooks. When it occurs in other documents, the additional details almost invariably turn out to be fabrications, and it is therefore a standing rule of historical criticism that successive layers of additional details are not acceptable as serious history. The layers of additional details in the prefaces of the surviving Welsh lawbooks are not exempt from that standing rule. We need for instance to keep a very open mind about Master Blegywryd. Since the statements in the prefaces that he was archdeacon of Llandaff and a Doctor of Laws are manifest fabrications, the parallel statement that he was the person chiefly responsible for drafting Hywel's lawbook must at the very least remain suspect, especially when we bear in mind that there is no satisfactory independent evidence that Blegywryd the lawyer even existed.

Side by side, however, with the layers of additional details the prefaces contain (as I have said) some passages which are common to all of them, common not only in substance but largely also in wording. It has been generally assumed, consciously or unconsciously, that what is called the ' unanimity ' of the prefaces about these common passages proves that at any rate the statements which those passages contain may be accepted as historically true. That assumption is not sound. In fact, all that the so-called ' unanimity ' of the prefaces proves is, not that the passages about which they are ' unanimous ' are to be accepted as true, but merely that those passages go back, directly or indirectly, to a common source, to a common original. The statements in that common original may have been true ; but equally they may not have been true : everything depends upon the character and quality of that common original. What was the common original of these prefaces ? It has been silently assumed in the past that the prefaces of the surviving Welsh lawbooks all go back, in regard to their common passages, directly or indirectly to the preface of Hywel's lawbook. But that assumption has never been critically examined, and we have no right to take for granted that such an untested assumption is necessarily sound. So far as we know at present, the common original of the prefaces to the surviving Welsh lawbooks may well have been, not the preface of Hywel's lawbook, but a preface concocted later than Hywel's time, quite possible as late even as the twelfth century, and very possibly concocted for a lawbook that was different from Hywel's, perhaps greater in length, and different in structure. That, however, is not a matter that can be pursued now.

The question from which this discussion started was — ' How far can we be sure that the Welsh laws were compiled by Hywel Dda ? ' My answer would be that we cannot, at present, be sure : not sure : not at present. Much more work needs to be done in the way of publishing the texts, and of analysing and comparing the structure, of the various surviving Welsh lawbooks. When we have learned much more about the existing lawbooks, the Welsh lawbooks as we have them, we may become more sure, one way or the other, about the alleged lawbook of Hywel Dda.

WALES ON THE EVE OF THE
NORMAN CONQUEST

By Glyn Roberts

THE Chronicle of the Welsh Princes — Brut y Tywysogion —
records that in the year 1043 there died " Hywel ab Owain,
King of Glamorgan, in his old age." It is not in itself a particularly remarkable entry ; but it gains some significance from
its context. During the century which precedes the Norman
Conquest of 1066, the chronicle is almost entirely a record of
feud and war. Between 949 and 1066 it refers to the deaths by
violence of some thirty-five Welsh rulers, either at the hands of
other Welsh kings, or at the hands of the English and the Danes :
four more were blinded, and yet another four were cast into
prison by their enemies. To add to the bald catalogue of
horrors, there were plagues which ravaged men and beasts ;
the piratical Danes descended on the coasts of Wales with
agonising regularity ; St. David's was sacked four times within
seventeen years, and one of its bishops was killed ; Welsh
captives by the thousand were carried off into slavery. In such
an age, the death of a Welsh king from mere old age was
perhaps deserving of particular mention.

To understand the history of Wales in this period, however,
something more is required than a summary of the more
depressing entries in Brut y Tywysogion. The death of Hywel
the Good in 950 — " the head and glory of all the Britons " as
he is styled by the chronicler — marked the close of a period.
We have already been shown that Hywel and his grandfather
— Rhodri the Great, who died in 878 — had both succeeded
in imposing something like political unity on the numerous
petty kingdoms of which Wales consisted. But in the case of
Hywel, as in the case of Rhodri before him, his death in 950
was followed by the division of his unified kingdom amongst
his descendants and his kinsmen. This failure to establish
lasting unity was the more tragic because the house of Rhodri

had won these partial successes in the teeth of difficulties which might well have daunted a less vigorous dynasty. During the eighth century the powerful English kingdom of Mercia was a continual threat along the eastern border ; the rise of Wessex to supremacy in the ninth century in no way lessened the danger. To add to the problems of the house of Rhodri, the coming of the Norsemen in the same period had exposed Wales, in common with the rest of western Europe, to those continuous attacks which, as we have seen, are so vividly reflected in the Welsh chronicle.

During the century with which we are immediately concerned, Hywel's descendants and kinsmen in Gwynedd, Powys and Deheubarth were engaged in the internecine feuds which were the result of the collapse of his kingdom — feuds which were complicated and exacerbated by warfare with English and Danes. And yet there is a pattern which emerges, despite the confusion. Much of the war and faction arose out of attempts by individual kings to re-establish the supremacy which had been enjoyed by Rhodri and Hywel. Of all Hywel's relatives, perhaps his grandson Maredudd ab Owain came nearest to repeating his achievement. For some thirteen years between 986 and 999 he ruled Deheubarth, Gwynedd and Dyfed, but he had to face the unceasing enmity of his dispossessed kinsmen in Gwynedd ; even his own nephew, Edwin ab Einon, did not scruple to call in the aid of the English of Mercia to harry the lands of his uncle in 992. Maredudd's death in 999 was the signal for renewed anarchy, but the Welsh chronicler recognised his significance and his quality when he described him as " the most praiseworthy king of the Britons " — a title, incidentally, which he had also bestowed on Rhodri the Great over a century earlier.

But it was typical of a period of anarchy that new men should appear on the scene — men, who, so far as is known, had little connexion with any of the existing dynasties. There was, for example, that Rhydderch ap Iestyn who ruled Deheubarth from 1023 to 1033. Again, a certain Aeddan ap Blegywryd, of quite unknown origin, succeeded for a while in maintaining himself in Gwynedd, only to be killed in 1018, with his four sons, by Llywelyn ap Seisyll, yet another pretender. He died in his turn in 1023. There can be no question that men of this type, despite the possible weakness of their hereditary claims, made a deep impression on popular memory. For example, the death of Llywelyn ap Seisyll in 1023 is marked in the Welsh chronicle by one of the few sustained pieces of prose which relieve the bald record of killing and violence. " And in his time," says the chronicler, " as the old men were wont to say, the whole land from one sea to the other was fruitful in men and in every kind of wealth, so that there was no one in want, nor anyone in need within his territory, and there was not one township empty or desolate." There is a curious similarity between this tribute to Llywelyn ap Seisyll in the Brut, and the comment of a Glamorgan scribe, writing about a century later, on the fame of Rhydderch ap Iestyn who died, as we have seen, in 1033—" in whose time " says the commentator, " there was no desert place in hill or plain, and but three townships left solitary in the whole of Wales." There can be no doubt that the colours in both pictures are too rosy, but in an age of confusion and uncertainty the strong man who could grasp power firmly, and wield it effectively, was naturally admired.

Yet another example of a Welsh strong man of this type deserves special mention, for he belongs to the years which immediately precede the Norman Conquest of 1066. Gruffydd ap Llywelyn ap Seisyll was the son of that Llywelyn ap Seisyll whose panegyric I have just quoted. In 1039, the reigning king of Gwynedd was killed by his own men and Gruffydd stepped into his shoes ; one authority, admittedly of doubtful reliability, implies that the new king had a hand in the death of the old. The Welsh chronicle, in recording his accession, summarises his career in these words : " from the beginning to the end, he hounded the Pagans and Saxons in many battles, and he prevailed against them, and slaughtered them and ravaged them," He does not mention that he hounded Welshmen, and slaughtered them, with equal efficiency. Certainly he dealt very effectively with the men of Mercia, but he also ruthlessly displaced his Welsh rivals. Walter Map, a native of Herefordshire who collected border legends and stories a century later, has preserved for us the grim witticism with which Gruffydd excused his removal of possible rivals from his path : " I kill no one", he said, "I merely blunt the horns of Wales, lest they should injure the mother." Gruffydd was not the man to die of old age, and he was not destined to found a dynasty. In 1063 he was overwhelmed by earl Harold, soon to ascend the throne of England, and Gruffydd was killed by his own followers. To the Welsh chronicler, he was " the head and shield and defender of Wales" , but his achievements, like those of his predecessors who had earned similar titles, did not outlive him. And although no one knew it at the time, his collapse differed from the others. Just three years after Gruffydd's death, far more dangerous enemies than Saxons or Danes were to land in Britain, and the danger to Welsh independence was to increase in intensity.

This is perhaps a convenient point in time at which to take stock, as it were, of this aspect of Welsh history up to this date. In the matter of the growth of political unity, there is a clear contrast between Wales and England. In England, the tendency from the beginning of the Anglo-Saxon period was for one kingdom after another to establish its supremacy, or at least its pre-eminence over the rest. By the eighth century, the dominant power was Mercia ; by the ninth century, it was Wessex. The threat from the Danes in the ninth and tenth centuries only had the effect of completing the process of unification. By the beginning of the eleventh century, therefore, political unity in England was a reality, and political institutions had developed a degree of complexity and efficiency not matched elsewhere in Europe. This unique character of English political development is the key to an understanding of the corresponding lack of such a development in Wales. The real question is not, " Why did Wales fail? " but " Why did England succeed ? " The explanation of the Welsh failure is not, I think, to be found in the strength of tribalism as a disruptive factor, although one must admit that the tribe, with its emphasis on family and kinship, did encourage local loyalties. Nor can the failure be explained by the Welsh practice of dividing private lands and kingdoms between all the sons of a proprietor or of a king. These features were not unknown in early Anglo-Saxon society, but they did not prevent unification. A more valid, though partial, explanation of Welsh disunity is geography ; the central upland and highland mass — the

" heartland " as geographers like to call it — certainly gave local particularism a physical basis. But, quite simply, the main reason for disunity in Wales was the close proximity of England. This is a platitude. It is equally platitudinous, and basically correct, to regard Welsh history up to 1282 as a continuous struggle against England for survival ; but the precise ways in which that struggle made for political disunity are worth looking at, very briefly.

Had it not been for the presence of the English on the eastern border, the conventional methods of power politics in Wales might well have solved her political problems ; that is, the strongest power would have absorbed the weaker. This, after all, was more or less what happened in England. The process of political unification there had progressed considerably before the coming of Norsemen or Danes served to complete it. In Wales, on the other hand, the first serious attempt at unification was made by Rhodri the Great in the ninth century, and it was made in the teeth, not only of the opposition of other Welsh princes, but also of English and Norse enmity from without ; it will be recalled that Rhodri met his premature death in 878 at the hands of the English. At no time therefore was it possible for Welsh internal affairs to be settled in isolation from external influences. The separate Welsh kingdoms were inevitably drawn into, and indeed joined willingly in, the complex manoeuvres which were made possible by the conflicts between English, Welsh, Norse and Danish. Not only did Welsh fight English ; English and Danes jointly ravaged Wales, Welsh in combination with Danes fought English, and Welsh kings were not slow to call in English or Danes against their fellow Welsh kings. In fact, examples can be quoted of all the possible combinations of all the available forces.

It is this political " realism " which is reflected in the succinct entries in the Welsh and other chronicles of the period. We know but little of what the subjects of the Welsh kings thought of these manoeuvres, but it is fairly certain that many of them would have welcomed a more united Welsh policy — a policy which reflected a more " patriotic " or at least a more consistently anti-English attitude. One remembers, for example, the somewhat grandiloquent titles bestowed by Brut y

Tywysogion on those Welsh rulers who did succeed in imposing temporary unity on the country. We should remember, too, the contents of one of the few Welsh poems which have survived from this troubled period — that *Armes Prydein* to which Professor Caerwyn Williams referred earlier. It is, in fact, a propaganda poem, written probably about the year 930 by a south Wales cleric. It appeals for an alliance between the Welsh, the Picts, the men of Cornwall and Strathclyde, and the Danes of Dublin, in an effort to expel the Saxons from Britain. It gains added point from the fact that the author must have been a subject of Hywel the Good, who was at that very time pursuing a consistent policy of friendship and co-operation with the kings of Wessex. In the year 937, Athelstan of Wessex crushed at the battle of Brunanburgh a confederacy of the kings of Scotland and Strathclyde with the Danes of Dublin, and it is very probable that *Armes Prydein* was written in support of this project. Hywel the Good was attending Athelstan's court during these very years ; and, whatever basis there may have been for the hope expressed by the author of *Armes Prydein*, the influence of Hywel may well have been the reason why Wales did not join the alliance. Such dreams of co-operation against England were not realistic. The tendency, in fact, was always in the direction of closer involvement with England. Marriage between Welsh kings and English princesses was not unknown. It is said that Cadwallon, king of Gwynedd, who was killed in 634, married a sister of king Penda of Mercia ; at the other extreme of our period, Gruffydd ap Llywelyn ap Seisyll married about 1050 the daughter of his ally, Aelfgar, earl of Mercia. The Welsh language itself reflects English influence, and the variety of borrowings from Anglo-Saxon implies very close contacts in many different fields.

One final and logical result of these relationships between Wales and England remains to be mentioned. By the ninth century — and possibly earlier — Welsh kings were being forced into formal subordination to English kings. The earliest known cases belong to the years after the death of Rhodri the Great in 878. The few Welsh kings whose territories had not been absorbed by Rhodri's acquisitive dynasty placed themselves under the protection of Alfred of Wessex, then at the height of his power and prestige; within a few years, Rhodri's own sons found it expedient to do the same. The precedent thus set was followed with some regularity in the tenth century, and Hywel the Good in particular made fealty to the kings of Wessex the main element in his policy. Even Gruffydd ap Llywelyn ap Seisyll, that scourge of the border English, swore to be faithful to Edward the Confessor in 1056 in return for confirmation in his gains : when he was finally overthrown by earl Harold in 1063, his possessions were divided among his successors on condition that they swore fealty to the Confessor. It is true that this well established feudal pattern could only be maintained by English kings by continual vigilance, and the periodic use of force. But it proved in the long run to be a fatal obstacle to any programme of political consolidation in Wales.

THE NORMAN CONQUEST

By William Rees

IN THE preceding pages we have seen Wales in the post-Roman era emerge, to acquire a distinctive pattern of culture and custom which for the first time we can regard as recognisably Welsh. Mountain and valley, however, kept the country divided and although elements of unity were present and Welshmen were learning to spreak of themselves as *Cymry*, or compatriots, there was as yet no thought of Wales as a political whole. Life was intensely local, and man's first allegiance was to his immediate family or clan and to his ruler of one or other of the petty kingdoms into which Wales was then divided. It was this absence of unity which made Wales a prey to the invader.

The Normans were but the last of the invaders into Britain from the Continent, bringing with them in turn new ways of life and thought to contribute to the sum of our civilisation. In the more accessible lowlands of the south and east of Britain, the blend of foreign and native elements could proceed unchecked, but in distant Wales, looking towards the western ocean and sheltered by its mountains, native life remained relatively unaffected by the new influences. Nevertheless, in the case of the Norman, so far-reaching was the impact of his coming, that even in Wales it left a deep imprint on the course of the development of the country. It was the Norman who introduced large-scale farming into Wales, also towns and trade, features virtually non-existent in pre-Norman Wales. He also reorganised the ancient Church of Wales on territorial and diocesan lines, to link it to Canterbury and to bring it more fully into the ambit of the Church of western Christendom.

We can hardly speak of a Norman conquest of Wales in the sense of a unified campaign directed by early Norman kings as part of a scheme of expansion into Wales. Rather did it consist of a number of isolated invasions by Norman lords who with their private armies sought to seize for themselves lands in Wales, beyond the English frontier. Only later was the king himself involved. It was the grant by William the Conqueror of the earldom of Hereford to his kinsman, William Fitzosbern, in the year following Hastings which constituted the first real threat to Wales and soon the castles of Wigmore, Clifford and Ewyas Harold marked the line of the southern border. Within a few years all Archenfield (south-west Hereford) had been annexed, its Welsh population retaining their ancient customs intact. This was followed by an incursion into southern Gwent (Monmouthshire), Fitzosbern setting up a castle at Strigoil (Chepstow) as the centre for his new lordship of that name, the first castle to be established on Welsh soil. Shortly afterwards, an advance further westward along the Roman road led to the establishment of the castle and lordship of Caerleon, whose history during the medieval period assumes an importance only secondary to that of Roman days. Beyond Hereford, and further north along the border, the Conqueror in 1070 established Roger of Montgomery as earl of Shrewsbury and Hugh of Avranches as earl of Chester and, just as today Hereford, Shrewsbury and Chester serve as the railway junctions for entry into Wales, so in those early days did they serve as bases for invasion. Robert gave his name to the castle of Montgomery which he built to prepare for his advance into central Wales. Hugh of Avranches moved from Chester into Flintshire, preparatory to the conquest of north Wales by his lieutenant, Robert of Rhuddlan, who took his name from the castle which he built on the banks of the Clwyd at Rhuddlan on the site of a former court of the Welsh rulers of north Wales. Afterwards he moved along the coast route to found a castle at Degannwy at the mouth of the river Conway. The way was made easier by civil war among the Welsh, which drove the legitimate rulers of north and west Wales, Gruffydd ap Cynan and Rhys ap Tewdwr, to take refuge in Ireland. In 1081 they returned to claim their own but Gruffydd was captured by Robert, who thereupon seized Gruffydd's lands of Gwynedd, setting up castles along the coast of north Wales even as far as Caernarfon, where an early castle, the primitive forerunner of the present massive pile, was built. It looked as if all north Wales would soon fall to the invader.

Such was the position at the close of the reign of William the Conqueror in 1087, but on his death events moved rapidly, and within a few years south Wales was subjected to concentrated attacks from Norman barons of the border. Philip de Braose moved into Radnor and then into Buellt. Bernard de Newmarch advanced into Brycheiniog, converting this sub-kingdom into the Norman lordship of Brecon. Normans also occupied Ewyas (Longtown), Monmouth and Abergavenny. From Gloucester, Robert Fitzhamon crossed the Severn estuary to the conquest of Morgannwg, defeating the last ruler, Iestyn, and establishing the lordship of Glamorgan. From central Wales the family of Montgomery overran Ceredigion (Cardiganshire) to establish itself in south-west Wales in the lordship of Pembroke. Large parts of Wales were passing out of Welsh control and the position seemed lost when at the opening of the twelfth century king Henry I confiscated the Shrewsbury earldom and the lordship of Pembroke, to implant himself in west Wales and to establish his first royal castle at Carmarthen. The seriousness of the situation roused the Welsh to widespread revolt and, by furious and concerted action, they drove the Normans to the shelter of the castles, recovering large tracts of the more remote and mountainous parts of the country. Their great opportunity, however, came on Henry's death in 1135 when, with the outbreak of civil war in England between Stephen and Matilda for succession to the throne, the Welsh under skilful leadership again made a great attack on the whole Norman position, recovering their hold over all the north and much of the west of the country, leaving to the Norman the lordships in the more accessible regions of the south-east and the coastlands of the south even as far as Pembroke. It was roughly along this dividing line between north-west and south-east Wales that a balance of power was for the first time established, enabling the still remaining independent kingdoms of Gwynedd, Powys and Deheubarth under their respective rulers to build up their defence and to postpone for well over a century the final loss of Welsh independence.

In each area the method of conquest at this early period

followed much the same pattern. A closely ordered troop of mailed knights and men-at-arms, horse and foot would force their way through the wooded country, often along the Roman roads, harassed on all sides by the Welsh. A close engagement to achieve quick and decisive victory was rarely possible, and the invaders would be driven to set up hastily a fortified enclosure on a defensible site which would allow of the throwing up of an earthen mound surrounded by a moat, the mound itself being capped by a wooden palisade to protect the wooden buildings in the interior. Such an open ' shell ' keep was by far the most common type of early castle in Wales and only in relatively few cases do we meet the rectangular stone towers generally found in England. Not until about 50 or 100 years later was the wooden ' shell ' reconstructed in stone, and many more years were to elapse before this was replaced by the powerful round-tower castle designed to counter the more advanced tactics by that time employed by the Welsh for the reduction of castles by the use of catapults, mangonels and other kinds of siege ' engines.'

A castle, once erected, served as a base of operations against the local Welsh ruler, giving cover in defence and providing economy in man-power, but after the fall of the ruler the fort would become the chief castle of the Norman lord for the defence of his newly-acquired territories, now to be administered on the feudal pattern of a Norman lordship. Knights in the train of the lord were rewarded by the grant of confiscated lands, giving rise to sub-lordships held by military tenure, the knight undertaking to serve in the army of the chief lord, in full armour and with barded horse, or to do garrison duty at the chief castle, for a period of 40 days, for each knight's fief at which in terms of feudal serive his estate was assessed. Each knight within his own lesser estate assumed the status of a petty lord setting up his own castle and manor and governing his tenants through his own courts. These military tenures of former days form the basis of many of the country estates of today.

In picturing the situation set up in the great Norman lordships of the march of Wales, we recall that these lordships had their origin not by grant of the English king but by force of private arms. On the defeat of a Welsh king, the Norman assumed the royal powers of that king, including the right of life and death over his subjects convicted in his courts, rights which in England were vested in the crown. The privileged position enjoyed by these Norman barons in their Welsh territories is further seen in the fact that while they owed allegiance to the English king, the king had little right to intervene in a lordship, except in certain specific circumstances, or to interfere in the succession. It was the possession of these special powers which distinguished a lord of the march from a feudal lord in England.

The castle of the lordship was not only a place of defence, as we so frequently think of it. It was also the headquarters of the government, containing the lord's chancery, for the administering of his affairs, and the exchequer, to which all rents and customary exactions levied by his bailiffs and other accounting officers were paid. It served, too, as the main court of the lordship where were tried offenders against the law, and here also was the gaol for their detention. Under the Welsh king, living among his own people, the royal centre had been opened and undefended, but the Norman lord could maintain his authority only behind strong walls. It was not the purpose of the Norman by his conquest to destroy or, indeed, to disrupt unduly the social life of the inhabitants, for such action, in jeopardising the very sources of revenue, would be economically suicidal. The greatest changes occurred, not unnaturally, along the main valley routes and in the fertile lowland parts of the lordship where trade and agriculture, familiar in the pattern of Norman life, offered prospect of success. This part of the lordship thus became the region of foreign settlement, the Englishry (as it was known), and here great open fields were cleared from the wooded waste for cultivation by the lord and his unfree tenants, including any Welsh unfree who happened to live in the immediate vicinity. These, the serfs of the lord, following the customary manorial practice, held their share of the arable as scattered strips in the open fields, in return for which they provided much of the labour for the working of the lord's share, the demesne.

Immediately outside the castle and under its protection

arose the borough, to which all trade in the lordship was confined to ensure the collection of the tolls. Here the burgesses, at first entirely of non-Welsh extraction, formed a foreign community, being induced to settle by the grant of the lord's charter which gave them a monopoly of trade and the privilege of self-government in their own court and by their own elected officers, the bailiffs or reeves, chosen for the year by their fellows. Within the town, each burgess, whether he be cooper or cordwainer, mercer or haberdasher, had his own site on which he built his house of wood, each trade often occupying a particular street. Normally, only burgesses, full members of the gild merchant, had the right to sell in the town, but at the weekly market the local country folk could bring in their produce to sell in the street upon payment of a small toll, while, during the period of the fair, trade was thrown open for as much as a fortnight when pedlars and packmen, acrobats and jugglers came from afar to set up their stalls in the streets or to entertain the crowd, after which they moved on to the next fair. For these itinerant strangers, the *pieds poudrés* or dusty feet, as they were called, a special court of the fair was held daily to deal with disputes or with offences against the bye-laws of the town concerning the prohibition of trading outside the official hours, the selling of inferior goods or the giving of short measure.

The Church in such a Norman setting soon lost some of its Celtic features and even the name of its Welsh saint, whether Padarn or Illtud, would give place by re-dedication to St. Mary or St. John or other saint of the Roman Church, and the church itself with its parish would be brought within the new diocese under a Norman bishop, the incumbent drawing his emoluments from the tithes and offerings of the parish. Or the lord, to win a blessing on his conquest, might assign the church and its parish to some English or continental abbey from which would come a few monks to found in the lordship a priory of the abbey, rebuilding the church in the Norman architectural style and setting up alongside of it and around the cloister the domestic quarters — the frater and dorter (refectory and dormitory) — to house the community of monks who set themselves apart not to preach but to minister to the glory of

God by prayer and fasting. Soon the new monastic house became the recipient of gifts from all sides, gifts of lands and fishing rights, of wine and wax, gifts of food from the castle and from the produce of the hunt, gifts of tithes, the tenth part of the produce of increase from lambs and calves and from corn and crops, or in certain cases an entire parish would be granted to the priory to swell the revenues, the monks appointing a paid vicar to conduct the services. Great might be the influence of such a house, the tolling bell a continual reminder of the call to prayer, the open door of the almonry and the guest house a solace for the poor and the wayfarer.

Outside this region of the Englishry was the surrounding hill country occupied by the main body of the Welsh who carried on their old mode of life in their widely scattered homesteads, pasturing their cattle, goats and swine, paying their old and accustomed dues, partly in money or more generally in kind to the new lord. This in many lordships took the form of a fixed contribution of cattle from the entire Welsh community, a contribution known as the *Commorth Calan Mai*, the *commorth* (or aid) of the first of May, usually in alternate years. This section of the population, the Welshry, held their lands according to Welsh custom, their local affairs being conducted in the separate Welsh courts in which Welsh law was administered much as of old.

In each of the Norman lordships of Wales we find this dual community, Anglo-Norman and Welsh, for, in the conduct of the courts of the lordship, separation provided the best answer for the governing of two hostile peoples living alongside yet differing so widely in outlook and custom. In some lordships the English section was extensive while in others it was confined to little more than the immediate manor and the borough. Only by the slow process of change through many centuries have the two peoples been brought together to share a common mode of life and a common system of administration, a process accelerated by the Act of Union of 1536 and the reorganisation of the country into shires on the English model.

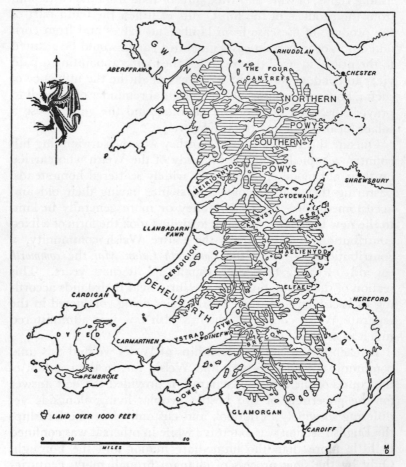

Wales before 1284. The dotted line shows
the present-day boundary of Wales

THE WELSH AWAKENING

By I. Ll. Foster

' THE Norman conquest of England', we have been told, ' (was) followed by Norman conquests in Wales ' and these conquests, as we have seen, were accomplished piece by piece. The units of penetration were the commotes, and with the possession of the commote went its lordship and everything which that meant : its royal character, its power of jurisdiction and its right of levying war and of plunder (*anrhaith*). My task is to give a straightforward account of the more vigorous and more sustained resistance of the Welsh to this Norman penetration, to these conquests, in the twelfth century. In this account my debt to Sir John Edward Lloyd's authoritative survey of the period will be immediately apparent.

First of all, let us remind ourselves of the main features in the immediate background. Dr. William Rees has explained to us how the earls whom William the Conqueror had established in Chester, Shrewsbury and Hereford laid down the pattern of Norman advances into Wales. Apart from his expedition to south-west Wales in 1081, the king seems to have left the conquest of Wales to his earls and barons. In 1087, the year of the Conqueror's death, Gruffudd ap Cynan, the prince of Gwynedd, whom that mistress of *brut*, Tangwystl, is said to have clothed with the garb of Gruffudd ap Llywelyn, was in bondage in earl Hugh's castle at Chester. The marks of penetration were already becoming clear in Powys and seemed likely to spread to Ceredigion. In the south-east, the boundaries of Brycheiniog and Elfael and of the kingdom of Morgannwg were for the moment left intact. And in Deheubarth there was Rhys ap Tewdwr.

Within a few years the castles of the earl of Chester could be seen along the Menai Straits at Caernarfon, Bangor and Aberlleiniog. Then, in 1093, Rhys ap Tewdwr was killed. We

can still sense the desolate grief and paralysing fears of Deheubarth in the sombre Latin verses of Rhigyfarch's lament : this
was *Dies Irae* indeed, and the Welsh had received their own
version of Doomsday.   Soon, Ceredigion and Dyfed were in
Norman hands.   In Powys, Brycheiniog, Ceredigion, Dyfed
and Deheubarth, Morgannwg and Gwent — the Normans
had come.

The revolt of 1094 led by Gruffudd ap Cynan, providentially
released from his captivity, and by Cadwgan ap Bleddyn of
Powys, married, incidentally, to the daughter of his Norman
neighbour Picot de Sai, sent the Normans back towards
Chester ; it swept in its course to Ceredigion and Dyfed and
made havoc of the new castles in the south except that of
Pembroke.

During the closing years of the eleventh century, then, there
were vigorous thrusts and counter-thrusts, and by 1100, the
beginning of the reign of Henry I, Gruffudd ap Cynan held
Anglesey, Cadwgan ap Bleddyn held Ceredigion and had a
portion of his heritage in Powys.   On the other hand, the
Normans held Rhos and Tegeingl — east of Conway — and
Brycheiniog, Glamorgan and Dyfed.

The events of the thirty-five years of Henry's reign looked as
if they would lead to the final subjugation and settlement of the
greater part of Wales by the Normans.   During the first fifteen
years Gruffudd ap Cynan succeeded in becoming the real
master of the region west of Conway.   Owain ap Cadwgan,
the dashing but embarrassing abductor of Nest, daughter of
Rhys ap Tewdwr and wife of Gerald of Windsor, this Owain
whose sins were so inequitably visited upon his father, had come
home from a second exile in Ireland to rule Powys.   Then, in
1114 Henry led a strong expedition against Gwynedd and
Powys.   Gruffudd ap Cynan understood the object of the
exercise ; he saw even though he did not taste the rod of chas-
tisement.   The outcome, as the Welsh Chronicle later tells us,
was that ' the king took him into his peace upon his paying him
a large tribute '.   As for Owain, who had gathered his men and
their chattels to the craggy safety of Eryri, Henry, with a touch
of ironical shrewdness, offered to take him to Normandy : ' and
I will make of thee a knight '.   And Owain was killed while on

active service for the king ; killed, as you remember, by a group of Flemings under Gerald of Windsor. Dyfed had received its colony of Flemings. Cadwgan ap Bleddyn had lost Ceredigion which now came into the strong hand of Gilbert FitzRichard of Clare. The king had a royal fortress in Carmarthen. And the picture was much the same eastward through Cantref Bychan, Cydweli and Gower to Monmouth. 'In the meantime', the Chronicle reports, ' there came a certain young man who was a son of the king of the South, to wit, the son of Rhys ap Tewdwr, whom some of his kinsmen had taken when a boy to Ireland ; and there he remained until he was a grown man. And at last tired of exile, he came to his own land, to Dyfed ; and his name was Gruffudd ap Rhys.'

But, in 1116, for Gruffudd ap Rhys and his young hopefuls eager for rebellion their day had not yet come, not least because political astuteness had made the ageing Gruffudd ap Cynan carry circumspection to the point of cynical opportunism—at least in his dealing with the son of Rhys ap Tewdwr at this time. Gruffudd ap Rhys before long came to terms with Henry, married Gwenllian, daughter of Gruffudd ap Cynan, and settled down in the commote of Caeo to enjoy Cantref Mawr.

I have suggested that Gruffudd ap Cynan of Gwynedd may have become more circumspect as he grew older. Circumspection, however, is not to be mistaken for timidity. Gruffudd, moreover, had sons by Angharad, daughter of Owain ab Edwin : they were Cadwallon, Owain and Cadwaladr. Together, father and sons brought Rhos and Rhufoniog, Meirionnydd and Dyffryn Clwyd into the control of the king of Gwynedd.

Henry I and Gruffudd ap Cynan and Gruffudd ap Rhys died within about two years of each other : Henry in 1135 and the two Gruffudds in 1137. But what forces were let loose between Henry's fatal surfeit of lampreys on the first of December 1135 and the pious death of Gruffudd ap Cynan and the untimely killing of Gruffudd ap Rhys in 1137 ? Henry, as I have said, died on the first of December. Stephen was crowned on the twenty-second of December 1135. On the very first day of January 1136 Hywel ap Maredudd, after a battle somewhere between Loughor and Swansea, marched into Gower. This was the beginning of the Welsh revolt, and the astonishing resurgence of Welsh aggressiveness between 1136 and 1154, that is during Stephen's reign, discloses both the nature of the forces let loose when Henry's strong grip was dropped and the skilful political exploitation of Stephen's weakness and difficulties. A flash point had been reached. The marcher lords almost to a man followed Robert of Gloucester in their support of the empress Matilda.

In 1136 Richard FitzGilbert was killed in an ambush near Crucywel. Cadwaladr and Owain, sons of Gruffudd ap Cynan, made three attacks on Ceredigion : in the second of these they were helped by Gruffudd ap Rhys. The outcome was that Cadwaladr held the northern half and Hywel ab Owain Gwynedd, warrior and poet, born of an Irish mother, took the southern half. Gruffudd ap Rhys drove into Dyfed before his death.

Gruffudd ap Cynan, as I have mentioned, made a pious death and he was mindful of his debt to Ireland. His biography, originally written in Latin towards the end of the twelfth century, closes with a picture of the Welsh ruler which reminds one of the Irish accounts of Brian Bóramha who died in the eleventh century : ' one who restores peace . . . to his people and rules with a strong hand in an ordered realm'. Under Brian ' the old literary tradition was revived and restored ' and one recalls the tradition which persisted until the sixteenth century of Gruffudd's reforming influence on Welsh poetic craft. In any case, it is significant that the earliest surviving example of the court poetry of the Welsh princes is Meilyr's elegy on Gruffudd ap Cynan.

Neither the death of Gruffudd ap Cynan nor that of Gruffudd ap Rhys slowed the pace and spread of Welsh confidence. Gruffudd ap Rhys had left four sons : Anarawd, Cadell, Maredudd and Rhys. Owain Gwynedd succeeded to the major share of the kingdom of Gwynedd. Owain Gwynedd began to extend and consolidate his possessions. Consolidation had perforce to mean the elimination of rivals : his brother Cadwaladr, accessory to the murder of Anarawd and husband of Alice de Clare, daughter of Richard FitzGilbert, having lost both north Ceredigion and Meirionnydd, was finally driven into exile in England ; Madog ap Maredudd of Powys, husband of Owain's sister, aided though he was by the earl of Chester, was also temporarily put out of action. By 1153, Owain's progress had brought Chester nearer to him.

In December 1154 Henry fitz Empress was crowned Henry II of England, but from January 1156 until April 1157 he was away in France. On his return to England he turned his attention to Wales : there he saw a young boy of ten as earl of Chester and Owain Gwynedd in vaunting power and dangerously near. Henry decided to protect the weak and to bring down the mighty. With Cadwaladr and Madog ap Maredudd to help him on land, a fleet of ships was to sail from Pembroke to join his land forces at Rhuddlan or Degannwy. The opposing armies engaged between Clwyd and Dee. The military issue was not decisive. Gwalchmai, the son of Gruffudd ap Cynan's poet Meilyr, who had earlier sung of Owain's attack on Ceredigion in 1136–8, has vividly described what happened at Tal Moelfre when Henry's naval arm was made powerless : ' and Menai ebbed not for the flood of blood that flowed ; and the salt sea grew red with men's gore.' The political result of the campaign of 1157 was that Owain paid homage to Henry and became ' prince' instead of ' king ' of Gwynedd ; the lands between the Clwyd and Dee were given up ; and Cadwaladr was restored to his possessions. For the next seven years Gwynedd was comparatively quiet, although Owain carried on resistance on what I may call the ecclesiastical front. In 1139 Owain and Cadwaladr had objected to Maurice bishop of Bangor taking the oath of fealty to the English crown when he professed obedience to Canterbury, and they were prepared to support the claims of Bernard of St. David's for metropolitan rights. For sixteen years after Maurice's death in 1161 the diocese of Bangor was without a bishop because of Owain's insistence on his rights in the election and appointment of the bishop.

Meanwhile, in Deheubarth, after the deaths of Anarawd and Maredudd, and the withdrawal of the wounded Cadell, Rhys ap Gruffudd had assumed leadership. At first he resisted Henry but in 1158 he came to terms with him. Rhys nominally

no longer ' prince ' of Deheubarth but henceforth 'the Lord
Rhys ' was permitted to keep Cantref Mawr and some small
oddments.   Ceredigion and Cantref Bychan were again in
Norman hands, but the Norman castellans were not given
much rest.   Rhys made an unsuccessful bid for Dyfed.   In
1162 he left the expensively built castle at Llandovery in ruins.
This contumacious breaking of oaths and agreements clearly
had to be stopped, and Henry II, progressing without much
trouble through Glamorgan and Gower, reached Pencader,
where Rhys, now politically wiser, surrendered, and did
homage at Woodstock.   Soon he was home at Dinefwr again
as arrogant and as restless as ever.   Within a short time he was
attacking Ceredigion, and of the many castles in that land that
of Cardigan alone was left in Norman hands.   This was in 1164.
In October of that year, at the Council of Northampton, the
quarrel between the English king and Thomas Beckett ended
in the archbishop's flight from England.   Even so, Henry was
not unmindful of Wales and at this same Council he was
promised a force of soldiers who would be tough enough for the
rigours of warfare on difficult Welsh terrain.   This time, however, if he decided to march, Henry would have to meet both
Owain Gwynedd and Rhys ap Gruffudd together, for Owain
had joined the revolt of Deheubarth.   Madoc ap Maredudd of
Powys, Rhys's father-in-law, was now dead.   His sons, his
brother Iorwerth Goch, and his nephew, Owain Cyfeiliog,
son-in-law of Owain Gwynedd and a remarkable example of a
' renaissance ' figure — all these, as well as the men of the
lands between the Wye and Severn, were now ready to join
their forces with those of Gwynedd and Deheubarth.   Owain
Gwynedd, without a doubt, was their prince and leader.

By May 1165 the stage was all set, but the drama had begun
a little earlier than Henry had expected.   Dafydd ab Owain
Gwynedd — offspring of that uncanonical marriage between
his father and Christina and later to marry Emma of Anjou,
half-sister of Henry II — Dafydd raided east of the river Clwyd
and brought back substantial plunder to Dyffryn Clwyd.
Rhuddlan and Basingwerk were in imminent danger.   Then
in July Henry ' with a host beyond number,' as the Chronicle
tells us, 'of the picked warriors of England, Normandy and
Flanders and Gascony and Anjou and all the North and

Scotland ' came to Oswestry purposing to destroy all Welshmen ! The Welsh forces encamped at Corwen. The two armies
stood poised for battle. Henry made the first important move.
He ascended the Berwyn range. And that was all. Rain,
floods and wind halted his advance and his supplies dwindled.
At sea the failure of his naval mercenaries was a wretched anti-
climax. Henry had no choice but to return to England, his
tempestuous nature no doubt raging more fiercely than the
storms which had swept his grand design scattering eastwards
from Berwyn.

During the next two years Owain Gwynedd destroyed the
castles of Basingwerk and Rhuddlan, and his authority was
firmly wielded as far as the Dee. In Powys, however, the
enthusiasm of Iorwerth Goch and Owain Cyfeiliog for the
Welsh cause did not last long. Memories of Madog's distrust
of Gwynedd and a realistic assessment of marcher conditions
directed their deeper allegiance to the English side. As for
Rhys ap Gruffudd, he finished what was to be done in
Ceredigion and came to hold Ceredigion, Ystrad Tywi and
Dyfed. He endowed and succoured the new Cistercian houses
which were thoroughly Welsh from their beginning in *pura
Wallia* or Wales proper. And the *clas* at Llanbadarn could still
look to him as its protector.

Owain Gwynedd died in 1170 : ' the man who was of great
goodness and passing great nobility and prudence, the strength
of all Wales ' in the words of the Chronicle. After his death,
the strife among his sons led to civil war. For the next quarter
of a century the personality of Rhys ap Gruffudd of Deheubarth, *yr Arglwydd* Rhys, dominates Welsh affairs. He had
taken the measure of Henry's strength. Furthermore, after
Beckett's death in 1171 the English king had his hands full of
worries at home and on the Continent. In particular, some of
the Norman adventurers in south-west Wales, among them
grandsons of Rhys ap Tewdwr, had been so successful in their
Irish enterprise as to alarm Henry their overlord, and to make
him seek a closer friendship with Rhys. Thus did stiff resistance
bring its sweet rewards. Rhys was formally recognized in his
possessions and made ' Justice ' of Deheubarth. He was now
an elder statesman and led the delegation of Welsh lords who
conferred with their English over-lord at Oxford in 1177 —

Dafydd ab Owain Gwynedd, Owain Cyfeiliog, Gruffudd ap Madog ap Maredudd. Henceforth, the middle-aged Rhys was unwavering in his loyalty to Henry and his beneficent authority exercised from his civilized court within the reconstructed castle at Cardigan was dominant over Deheubarth until Henry's death in 1189.

It has been said that Richard I, the Lion-heart, ' was the least English of all kings of England ' ; during his ten years' reign he spent six months in all in England. The relationship between Rhys ap Gruffudd and Henry II in many ways had been a personal one. With the accession of Richard the old spirit of revolt possessed Rhys once more and he waged war on his neighbours. But he was no longer the resourceful purposeful campaigner of earlier days. And his ebbing vigour was further weakened by strife among his sons. He died in 1197. The twelfth century was drawing to its close. The resistance of Owain Gwynedd and Rhys ap Gruffudd to deeper Norman penetration had not prevented the principle of Anglo-Norman lordship over Wales from being asserted and partially accepted, but the struggle had prevented the whole of Wales from becoming a patchwork of Anglo-Norman lordships and the leader who was soon to take over from Owain and Rhys would firmly grasp the reason why they had so vigorously resisted being made ordinary feudal lords.

THE POETS OF THE PRINCES

By D. Myrddin Lloyd

Saxon England fell to the Normans at a blow, but in Wales there was a dogged struggle of two centuries, with violent swings of the pendulum. Our subject is the poetry of the bards who were attached to the courts of the native princes of the twelfth and thirteenth centuries. The *pencerdd*, or chief court poet, sat next to the king's or prince's heir, and next to the judge, while the *bardd teulu*, or poet of the household, had his seat next to the captain of the household guard. The *pencerdd* had not only to magnify the fame of his prince, but to perpetuate certain ideals which gave meaning to the organised life of the Welsh community, the *bardd teulu* performing a similar function usually in a simpler style, and addressing himself more to the womenfolk of the court and to the household troops. Both functions could be fulfilled by the same poet.

In later periods Welsh poets were sometimes charged with obsequiousness and falsehood in their praise of patrons, and probably rightly so, but there is a quality about much of the poetry of the twelfth and thirteenth centuries which rings true. Cynddelw, greatest of twelfth-century court poets, was not alone in claiming that poetic talent was a gift from God which was not to be debased (" *Difreiniaw dawn Duw, nid dyn a'i medd*"). The relationship of prince and poet is often likened to *carennydd* (kinship) — a bond of profound significance. The leading poets did not hesitate to remind the princes how much they needed each other. Relations could become strained, and the poet might have to plead for forgiveness, but he knew how to do so without servility. Cynddelw is capable of facing murmurs of opposition with the proud words : " You, court silencers — get me silence. Quiet, poets ! you are about to hear a poet ! " Bards could speak plainly of their right to choose whom they would serve, and some of them did not hesitate to criticise the oppressiveness of even the most powerful rulers. When Llywelyn the Last imprisoned an unruly brother he had to face the criticism of a poet who reminded him of a higher sanction than his own princely will and power (" It pertains only to God to deprive a man of his due portion "). There is every indication that much of the court poetry of the twelfth and thirteenth centuries can be taken quite seriously as the poets' considered thoughts and feelings on the vital issues of their day.

These poets had a very clear conception of the meaning of their people's history and the significance of the events of their own day. The past and the present were mutually explicable as parts of the same pattern. Now we know from the chronicles that Welsh fought Welsh as often as they fought the invader, and that survival of native rule depended as much on subtlety as on valour, as much on the discovery of a fruitful compromise as on resistance. Alliances and intermarriage with Norman and English were part of the game, but all this is played down by the bards. Their outlook was moulded by the poetry of the heroic age of the sixth century — when Urien, his son Owain, Rhun, the Coelings, and the Gododdin had striven against the Brynaich and the Deifr — Bernicians and Deirans — Angles of Northumbria, whose kingdoms had long been absorbed into Saxon and, later, Norman England. French-speaking followers of the Conqueror and their descendants were still the *Brynaich* to the poets — it was still the same age-old struggle. Although Welsh princes of the twelfth and thirteenth centuries were sometimes likened to biblical and classical heroes, and to Arthur, the prevailing comparisons were to the old northern heroes and there is frequent harking back to the old place-names, Din Alclud (Dumbarton), Arfderydd and Carlisle. " The Old Song of Taliesin", we are assured, " is new for countless years." In the rise of new and powerful princes poets see the return of Cynan and Cadwaladr — a prophesied restoration of the right order of things. The seer Myrddin had proclaimed that these things were to be. This outlook or faith spread by the poets gave an exaltation to all who were moved by it, but it also imposed a pattern within which contemporary events and issues were seen — highlighting certain features and obscuring others, and providing a driving-force which could lead to victory or to ruin.

There is another aspect of the bards' attitude to history and the course of events. We have learnt to stress the impersonal — economic factors, natural resources, geography, legal systems. It is also true that the Welsh under their native princes were far from blind to these things. They exulted in their enlightened laws and privileges, the household troops knew their terrain, movable wealth mainly in the form of cattle was coveted ; and all this was reflected in the poetry, but the poets placed the personal qualities of the leader and the household troops far higher than all these. On the death of Madog ap Maredudd in 1160 Powys met a sad reversal of fate. "Privileges," laments Cynddelw, " are now barren things." During these two centuries of dramatic events and precarious freedom it was brought home time and again to poet and community how much depended on the courage and the coolness of judgment of the ruler. " In the vale of Llangwm I contemplated my ruler, and what I sang will be contemplated." The ' contemplation of rulers' was the métier, the business, of these poets, and they sensed its vital significance in the given circumstances.

Welsh poetry of the fifteenth century is full of absorbing detail about houses, clothes, gardens, horses and craftsmanship, but the concentration of interest in our period on rulers and their entourage means there is far less of this. Such details do however occur.

We read of a sword of three meltings, and of the glass windows through which the court ladies peep with admiration at Cynddelw the fine fellow. We catch a glimpse of the church of Henfynyw amidst its clover and oaks, and Bleddyn Fardd tells us of the green tents used by the host of Llywelyn the Last —an interesting instance of camouflage. Glimpses are caught of the studious and quiet life of the *clas* — the ecclesiastical community forming an island of calm, such as that of the church of Cadfan at Towyn in Merioneth. It is noteworthy that some poets felt drawn to these seats of piety and learning ; for instance, in the words of Einion ap Gwalchmai, " Weary am I of the service of princes . . . Blessed are they, monks in churches."

Our period saw great religious activity in Wales. Indigenous cults, particularly thac of David, maintained their appeal, and were given a new significance by the national revival. At the same time the Welsh princes were great patrons of the Cistercians, whose austere practices were to become so well established in the Welsh countryside at Aberconway, Valle Crucis, Cymer, Ystrad Marchell, Strata Florida, Whitland, Neath, Margam, and elsewhere. In the thirteenth century the influence of the preaching of friars was to spread. Religious influences are very pervasive in the work of the court poets. With stark emphasis on piety and purity, these odes do reveal that depths of very real religious feeling were being stirred. " *Anghrefydd ysydd ysywaeth* " (Irreligion prevails, alas!), laments Cynddelw, but this is a cry that was again much heard at the height of the methodist revival in the eighteenth century, and it would have been more ominous had there been no one there to utter it. In such unsettled times as the twelfth and thirteenth centuries it is not surprising that the religion of withdrawal and seclusion is often appealingly depicted. One thinks of the first Meilyr's deathbed poem with its lovely picture of Bardsey, the resting place of saints, and the contemplative verse of his grandson and namesake who wished to become " God's bard." However, poets then did also turn to God for strength, and there is frequent passionate religious protest against oppression even on the part of native princes — a protest based on the conviction that there is a natural order in God's creation on which the pride of man cannot infringe with impunity. There are sudden touches of profoundity as when the mystery of the Incarnation is conceived in terms of kinship, with its mutual obligations; " *Y Duwdod, undod undras â mi* " (The Deity, a unity one in kinship with me), God having assumed the obligations of kinship with man in becoming flesh.

Forays, skirmishes, and the activities of prince and young household warriors, however, have more place than religion. " In the field of Mathrafal the sods are trampled under the feet of proud horses." We live again a night raid on the Severn border in the words " We are welcomed with drink under stars and moon by a generous bloodstained warrior ; on

the Long Hill the tall powerful eagle, and on Severn the de-
lightful smile of men." Owain Cyfeiliog, prince and poet,
describes the return from a foray after break of dawn, " And
lo ! the long hillside and the valley were full of sun ! "

Delight in nature is keen, and is conveyed in sharp vivid
glimpses accompanied by poignancy of feeling. Usually it is
associated with the life of the community, and love of wildness
is unusual. Even prince Hywel ab Owain Gwynedd, who
loved the broad expanses of mountain and sea, soon returns to
the " settled parts" which are laden with memories of his own
folk. Much of the native poetry is interlaced with Welsh
place-names, and served to enhance a concrete awareness of
the homeland.

In Wales and Ireland it was a common practice for young
princes to be brought up, not in their parents' home, but by
foster-parents chosen from among the free-born families. The
staunch cameraderie between foster-brothers is well expressed
by Peryf ap Cadifor Wyddel, one of six foster-brothers to prince
Hywel ab Owain Gwynedd. " While we were seven, three
sevens dared not challenge us." He also reveals the unhappy
animosity liable to arise between separated natural brothers.
Poems like his are a valuable side-light on the upbringing of
princes.

Gerald of Wales once remarked how well it would be for the
Welsh if they had only one prince and that a good one. Others
too, besides Gerald, came to think so, and the court poetry
throws a fascinating light on the growth of this ideal and the
tensions which it created. It is true that twelfth century poets
speak of the country as if it were one "from the gate of Chester
to Port Skewet," but the unity consists in a common pattern of
society, similar laws and institutions, the use of the same
language, and the sharing of the same historical traditions.
There are hints, even by Meilyr, early in the twelfth century, of
the supremacy of Aberffraw over all other Welsh seats of
government, but it did not amount to much. Wales was
divided into a number of long-established principalities, and
certain poets feel that the integrity of these provinces had a
validity in the natural order. They reveal deep-seated
scruples. *Trais* (oppression) and *traha* (over-reaching, or
hubris) had long been feared as harbingers of divine retribution.

" We have had Arthur, Cæsar, Hercules, and Alexander, world ruler who was restless even to the signs of the zodiac. Why will not people see, through severe affliction, that all over-reaching is a pulling down, and a destruction, a rejection of the supreme Lord of all Scripture, and that to indulge in it is a striving against the right order of things ?"

The great internal political dilemma of twelfth- and thirteenth-century Wales was that the country needed unity, and that it could not be clearly seen how to attain unity with justice and general assent. We would have little inkling of the heartburning that this problem caused were it not for the poetry. Owain Gwynedd moved into Powys on the death of Madog ap Maredudd, but, says Cynddelw, " one should not hold anything in this world that does not come from God."

But the rising tide of Welsh patriotism demanded a new order. One stage is seen in the rule of the Lord Rhys, a *primus inter pares*, direct ruler of a large tract of the south, and exercising a regulative authority under King Henry over all other rulers in Wales, both Welsh and Norman. The Welsh in his day were able to raise their heads. Their language and poetry were endowed with prestige, upheld by the " Majesty of the South " (*Maiestawd Dehau*). No wonder the cult of David was extolled by one of Rhys's court poets — a cult indigenous in Rhys's own domain but influential throughout Wales. Gwynfardd Brycheiniog speaks of all the other saints at the synod of Brefi submitting to the wisdom and authority of David and, significantly at the height of the Plantagenet empire, the saints of Anjou, Brittany, England and the north show respect for him. Moreover, love of David had to be expressed in good Welsh ! Quite clearly the poet is seeking deep roots in Welsh tradition for the Lord Rhys's policy.

In the next century the two Llywelyns were to secure a much closer unity, and the claims of Aberffraw to supremacy over all other Welsh seats of government became practical politics. It is noteworthy that the poet Llywarch, Brydydd y Moch, anticipated Llywelyn the Great's policy of uniting as much of Wales as he could under his own rule in his verses to Dafydd ab Owain Gwynedd who never became strong enough to implement it. It is a clear instance of a poet helping to create an

attitude of mind conducive to the rise of a Llywelyn. Aberffraw was within Dafydd's petty domain at the time ; hence
for Llywarch he was the " *Prif deyrn canhwynawl* " (the prime
rule by inherent right). The poet reminds him that it was not
love that had got him that far, but his prowess in battle, and
that it behoved him to achieve a " *kadr heddwch* " (a strong
peace). But it was in Llywelyn the Great that Llywarch was to
find his ideal ruler. He exults in his hero's disregard for
frontiers. (" *Ac ar bob terfyn — torri*"). He turns the tables on
those who felt scruples, for Llywelyn's claims as lord of Aberffraw were inherent. It was not he who was guilty of *traha* but
those who withstood his claims ! " (*Traha yw i neb ni bo caeth
i'm rhwyf*"). The ripening national outlook of the day is seen
in Llywarch's appeal to the men of Powys : " Let the Powys
people realise who he is — the king of a strong people. Is it
better to have a Frenchman than a generous Welshman ? "
The new unity is presented as an ' uncovering ' (*dadanhudd*) of
the right order of things ; foretold by Myrddin it was the
removal of a *camwri* — a wrong state of affairs.

In the next generation the rise of the national spirit can be
traced through the work of Dafydd Benfras to its climax in that
of Llygad Gŵr who sang to Llywelyn the Last at the height of
his power from 1267 to 1277. He hails him as king of the
Welsh whose quarrel is with an " *estron genedl anghyfiaith* " (a
foreign nation of alien speech). The term Cymru Fawr (Great
Wales) is increasingly used, and the poet incites the second
Arthur to march even into Cornwall !

But ebb-tides of fortune were also experienced, and the poets
knew the " grindstone of anxiety " (*agal gofal*). Then all
the old scruples were gnawing at their hearts : " we have all
been too oppressive for a long while " complains Dafydd
Benfras when Gruffydd ap Llywelyn fell to his death in an
attempt to escape from the Tower of London.

The magnificent elegy of Gruffydd, son of the Red Judge, to
Llywelyn the Last whose death on that fateful December day in
1282 brought down the whole precarious edifice of native Welsh
rule, is unrelieved in its utter dismay. There must have been
many who felt like that. "Why are we left to linger ? " A
splendid poem, but I feel drawn rather to the more subtle and

braver poem by Bleddyn Fardd : " He who endures the profoundest grief let him be the steadiest. " Llywelyn is likened to Priam, and for the stock of Brutus ap Silvius there had been an unforeseen sequel to the fall of Troy. The poet then refers to Christ's vicarious suffering for mankind. Llywelyn too had been killed for others — for us. These are merely hints. They are not laboured but they are clearly there.

We today know that all was not lost. A numerous class of small property owners had been imbued with the ideals of the Welsh courts and came to assume leadership and to offer patronage. The support of monastic houses by the princes was to bring a rich reward in that these houses continued for centuries to maintain a strongly Welsh outlook and to support Welsh culture very effectively. And ere long the greatest poetic genius that Wales has yet produced was to appear on the scene, and to warm men's — and women's — hearts to the delights of Welsh poetry and song.

THE WALES OF GERALD

By Thomas Jones

EARLIER writers in this volume have told how the Norman invaded parts of Wales, how the Welsh halted the invaders, and how the bardic eulogies and elegies of the court poets reflect the achievements and aspirations of the Welsh princes. We shall now look at Wales and its inhabitants as they appeared, towards the end of the twelfth century, to Gerald of Wales, archdeacon of Brecknock and a lively writer in Latin.

Gerald was born about 1146 and died in 1223, after an eventful career during which he served the king, lectured in the University of Paris, twice came near to being elected bishop of St. David's, and visited Rome at least four times. His father was the Norman William de Barri of Manorbier and his mother was Angharad, daughter of Gerald de Windsor, another Norman lord. His maternal grandmother, Gerald de Windsor's wife, was the famous and beautiful Nest, daughter of Rhys ap Tewdwr, the last independent ruler of south Wales, who died in 1093. Well could Gerald say, ' I am sprung from the princes of Wales and from the barons of the Marches, and when I see injustice in either race I hate it.' On the Welsh side he was related to the powerful Lord Rhys, who ruled South Wales until his death in 1197, and to many of the minor princes of that land. On the Norman side he had family connections with the FitzGeralds and with Richard Strongbow of the great house of Clare. His mixture of Welsh and Norman blood made him appreciate and from time to time sympathize with the efforts of both Normans and Welsh in their struggle for ascendancy. He wrote so much about himself that he is better known to us as an individual than any other figure in mediæval Wales. His many books are, at the same time, a storehouse of information about Wales and its peoples as he saw them.

This is especially true of his *Itinerary through Wales* and his

Description of Wales. The *Itinerary* first appeared in 1191 and its central theme is the account of archbishop Baldwin's tour of Wales, during Lent of the year 1188, to preach the Third Crusade — a tour on which Gerald officially accompanied the archbishop. The journey from Hereford, via Cardiff, Swansea, Carmarthen, St. David's, Cardigan, Strata Florida and Llanbadarn to the river Dyfi, the boundary between north and south Wales, took over a month. The whole of north Wales, via Towyn, Nefyn, Caernarfon, Bangor and St. Asaph to Chester, and thence, via Oswestry, Shrewsbury, Ludlow and Leominster, back to Hereford, the starting point, was covered in eight days. Although there are occasional details which vividly light up certain scenes, the account of the journey as such is rather bare and impersonal. Amongst the vivid details we have the scene at Abergavenny where a man by the name of Arthen hesitated to enlist as a crusader until the archbishop scathingly asked him whether he first wished to take counsel of his wife, and that other scene in Anglesey where Rhodri ab Owain Gwynedd's retinue sat on a rock listening to Baldwin's address but remained unmoved by his eloquent appeal for recruits. Fortunately, Gerald could not resist wandering, not off the track followed by the archbishop, but in the wide fields of his own observations, thoughts and memories. His many and varied digressions, when brought together and analysed, amount to a guide to the topography, antiquities and politics of twelfth-century Wales and to the religious rites and customs, the superstitions and folk-tales of the inhabitants.

Gerald's second book on Wales, the *Description*, which appeared in 1194, is in form a sharp contrast to the *Itinerary* in that it is singularly well-planned and remarkably free from digressions. It is an objective and half-philosophical essay on Wales in four parts, each of them dealing respectively with its geography, the virtues of the Welsh, their faults and vices, and how the Normans can best conquer and govern the land and how the Welsh can best resist them.

Let us piece together the more important things we learn about Wales and its people from these two books — the digressive *Itinerary* and the planned and objective *Description*. Let us see what general picture emerges of the geography and topography of the country, of its politics including the clash between Welsh and Normans, of its religion and ecclesiastical movements, and of the general way of life of the inhabitants.

Wales is a land of high mountains and deep valleys, great forests, rivers and marshes, all of which have helped the Welsh to ward off conquest by English and Norman invaders. Its three main divisions are Gwynedd, Deheubarth and Powys, each with its respective main court at Aberffraw in Anglesey, Dinefwr, near Llandeilo, and Pen-gwern, near Shrewsbury. Each province is divided into cantrefs : there are twelve in Gwynedd, twenty-nine in Deheubarth, and six in Powys, with three of the latter in English and Norman hands. Most of the rivers flow from the two mountain ranges of Elenid (an old name for Plynlimon) and Eryri or Snowdonia, but some have their source in the mountains of Cantref Bychan (now called the Black Mountains), the Brecknock Beacons, the hills of Glamorgan and the mountains of Presely. The most attractive region is that around Cardigan, and in particular Dyfed, by virtue of its level plains and coastland. Gwynedd has the best natural defences, its land is rich in pasture, and it breeds men of great physical strength. The wildest land is Meirionnydd, with its rugged mountains traversed by shepherds, and its men are as expert with the long-spear as the men of the south, especially those of Gwent, are with bow and arrows. The soil of Anglesey is dry and stony, as unsightly as that of Pebidiog, near St. David's, but so incomparably more fertile in crops that one speaks proverbially of Anglesey as ' the mother of Wales ' —' Môn Mam Cymru'. At Caerleon Roman remains were to be seen within and without what was still standing of its once massive and unbroken city wall. Carmarthen, that other Roman stronghold, is surrounded by meadows and labyrinthine woods, and parts of its original brick walls are still to be seen. The Norman castle of Manorbier, Gerald's birthplace, with its fine turrets and ramparts, its fish-pond and orchard, its mill and church, is lyrically described as standing on a hill not far from the sea in the region which Gerald salutes as the loveliest in the whole of Wales. Gerald saw beavers on the river Teifi, and he watched the salmon leap the falls at Cenarth. Near St. David's the remains of a submerged forest were to be seen at low tide. The Welsh language, which so closely resembles Cornish and Breton, is purer, so Gerald tells, in the north than in the south, but some maintain that the best idiom is to be heard in Cardigan.

The political divisions correspond to the three main geographical divisions. There was no united Wales which enjoyed the rule of one prince. In south Wales we see the Lord Rhys, as justice under the king, wielding authority over a number of minor rulers, most of whom were related to him by blood or by marriage. Einion ab Einion Clud held Elfael, Maelgwn ap Cadwallon ruled in Maelienydd, Morgan ap Caradog, who guided the archbishop through the dangerous quicksands, held the land between the rivers Afan and Neath, and Hywel ap Iorwerth, who was partial to the English, ruled in Caerleon. Meirionnydd was in the hands of two brothers, Gruffudd and Maredudd, sons of Cynan and grandsons of the great Owain Gwynedd. Their uncles Rhodri and Dafydd, sons of that Owain, ruled Gwynedd, Rhodri holding Anglesey, and Dafydd most of the other part. In Powys there were several princes : in Upper Powys, Owain Cyfeiliog, who is known to us as a gifted poet, some of whose compositions are still extant ; and in Lower Powys, Gruffudd and Elisau, sons of Madog ap Maredudd who ruled all Powys when he died in 1160. Gerald draws a grim picture of endless feuds between all these leaders and others of lesser standing, and blames firstly the Welsh system of inheritance by which on the death of the father all the sons share the land equally, and secondly the custom of fosterage. His stories and reminiscences confirm his considered statement that the greatest weakness of the Welsh was their factiousness and the disunity which resulted from their refusing to acknowledge one supreme prince.

All the land, however, was not held by the Welsh. At Llandaff, we are told, two separate groups of people listened to the archbishop's sermon in 1188, the Welsh on the one side and the English on the other. Powys in particular had suffered considerably from aggression by the English. Other foreigners were the Flemings whom king Henry I had settled in Pembroke in the early years of the twelfth century. Despite their enmity towards the Welsh, Gerald praises them as ' a strong and powerful people', skilful in commerce, agriculture and war. In the marches, in the lowlands of Glamorgan, along the southern seaboard as far west as Pembroke, and in some places in the less accessible north, Norman lords had established themselves. They are revealed to us as ambitious adventurers playing their game of power politics and ever seeking to extend their territories and to consolidate their position by open war, by intermarriage with the Welsh, and by every other means fair and foul. Many of these Norman barons, some of them contemporaries of Gerald, appear in the *Itinerary*, generally in stories and reminiscences : Bernard de Newmarch, Hugh of Chester, Maurice de Londres, Robert de Belême, William de Breos, Richard de Clare, the FitzMartins, the FitzTancards, and the FitzAlans. In one story Gerald recounts the exploit of Ifor Bach of Senghennydd entering Cardiff castle, despite the close guard upon it, and carrying off William, earl of Gloucester, and his wife and son. This incident reflects the general attitude of the free Welsh in their mountain and forest fastnesses, towards the foreign invaders in their fortified castles. Presently we shall see how these Welsh lived, but first let us examine the religious and ecclesiastical scene.

The Welsh are devout Catholics who recognize the rule of Canterbury under the Pope. To counteract contemporary propaganda for the recognition of St. David's as a metropolitan see independent of Canterbury, Baldwin celebrates mass in the four Welsh cathedral churches. All the more important princes of Wales come to pay their respects to the archbishop with the exception of Owain Cyfeiliog of Powys, who is promptly excommunicated for this sin of omission. The Lord Rhys not only met the archbishop and his company on their entry into Wales but also later entertained them in his castle at Cardigan and then travelled with them as far as the river Dyfi. We hear of tithes, and pilgrimages, of fast, of penance, of the reverence shown to all kinds of saintly relics — horns, croziers and hand-bells — of absolution from sins, and of malediction and excommunication. At Llanbadarn, near Aberystwyth, the old Welsh *clas*, a church community half-secular and half-monastic, continued : and there, as in some other places, the offices of abbot and priest passed from father

to son. Gerald condemns this practice, as he does marriage
between cousins and the failure of some Welsh ecclesiastics to
observe celibacy. Many monasteries had been founded, most
of them Cistercian — Margam, Neath, Strata Florida, Aber-
conwy and Basingwerk — and there were Benedictine cells at
Ewenni and St. Dogmaels. There were monks on Bardsey
Island too, and hermits who lived by the labour of their hands
on the island of Priestholme. Practical man though he was in
matters of church and state, Gerald himself felt the attraction of
the peaceful life. He writes with warmth of feeling of the
' little place and home ' which, as archdeacon of Brecknock,
he had at Llanddew, near Brecon ; and he eloquently con-
trasts the poverty and purity of Llanthony abbey in the secluded
vale of Ewyas with the wealth and worldliness of the daughter-
monastery at Gloucester.

Lastly, let us look beyond the topographical, the political
and religious scenes and observe how the Welsh live from day
to day. They are all proficient in the use of arms, their defensive armour is slight, and most of the people fight on foot.
Their cultivation of the land is primitive, and their main diet
consists of meat, oats, milk, butter, and cheese. Generally
they are moderate eaters : and on a warlike expedition they
can go without food from morning till night. Guests are
everywhere hospitably received and entertained with music
on the harp. They sleep, in the scant clothes which they wear
by day, on a common bed of rushes spread along the sides of
the house. Both sexes cut their hair in a circle level with their
eyes and ears, and the women wear a white head-dress arranged
not unlike the eastern turban. They clean their teeth with a
green hazel twig and a piece of woollen cloth. Their musical
instruments are the harp, the pipes and the *crwth*. Bards, whose
compositions are full of alliteration and internal rhyme, are
numerous amongst them and are held in high esteem. To
entertain them they also have storytellers. The people sing,
not in unison, but in many voices, modes and keys which never
fail to harmonize. When they indulge in jokes and sarcasm
they often use puns, playing upon the meaning and form of
words. All alike have the gift of eloquence and can argue un-
afraid even in the presence of princes. When they have difficult

problems to resolve, they consult strange ecstatic soothsayers
called *awenyddion* whom Gerald learnedly compares with the
prophets of the Old Testament. Over and above everything
else they esteem purity of pedigree and noble ancestry. Even
those of low degree are most careful of their family trees and
they know them by rote through father, grandfather, great-
grandfather right back to the sixth and seventh generation, and
even beyond that. Their houses are built of woven osiers on
the edge of forests and they last but for a year. To draw their
rude ploughs and carts they use oxen yoked sometimes two,
but more often four abreast, whilst the man with the goad
walks backwards in front of them, singing as he goes. For
reaping they use the sickle, but more generally an implement
which appears to have been some primitive kind of scythe.
Their small and light coracles, nearly triangular in shape, are
made from osiers covered, on the outside of the framework,
with untanned skins. And fishermen carry them on their
shoulders to and from the rivers which they fish for salmon or
over which they want to pass.

As a people the Welsh have their faults as well as their
virtues. There are no better people to be found than their best
men, but their worst men are very bad. They tend to be un-
stable, treacherous, guilty of falsehood and perjury, and given
to robbery and plunder. As fighters they soon lose heart if
they are stubbornly opposed, and so they are better in guerilla
warfare than in pitched battles. Defeated one day, on the
morrow they will be ready to attack again. There are constant
feuds and litigations amongst them, often between brothers ;
they commit frequent murders, acts of arson, and fratricide ;
and in times of plenty, after long fasting and hunger, they can
indulge in gluttony. Gerald cannot accept their confident
belief that very soon, at the fated time sung by their prophets,
they will drive out the hated invaders and regain their old
supremacy over the whole island of Britain.

If the Normans are to conquer all Wales and rule it in peace
they must improve their strategy and tactics, and Gerald is
ready with advice of a most practical kind. But he also coun-
sels the Welsh how they can best avoid defeat ; and his advice
to them is warm and passionate when compared with the cold

Macchiavellian sagacity of his precepts to the Normans. Here at least the Welshman in Gerald proved stronger than the Norman in him and impelled him, in the concluding paragraph of the *Description*, to express in epic style the bold words which an unnamed Welshman spoke to King Henry 11 at Pencader in 1163. The words, as recorded by Gerald, are a token of the undaunted spirit with which the Welsh faced the Norman invasion and looked forward with confidence to the future. And the words were these :

> ' This nation, O King, as it deserves, may be oppressed and very largely destroyed and weakened through thy might and that of others, now as in days gone by and many times to come. Completely exterminated, however, it will not be through the wrath of man, unless it be that the wrath of God accompanies it. And no nation, so I deem, other than this of the Welsh, and no other language, upon the stern Day of Judgement before the Most-high Judge, will answer — whatever may happen to the greater remainder of it — for this little corner of the earth'.

THE AGE OF THE TWO LLYWELYNS

By T. Jones Pierce

By the close of the twelfth century, as we have been told, Norman power had been permanently established over large parts of south Wales. The consequent dichotomy which divided Wales into two spheres of political influence — Norman and Welsh — is a feature of Welsh political arrangements which was carried over into the thirteenth century ; and, indeed, it is a feature which, in modified form, continued to influence the course of Welsh history down to the union of England and Wales in 1536. As in the age of Gerald, so in the age of the Llywelyns, one must retain in the mind's eye the contrast between the marcher lordships, extending in a broad arc between the palatinates of Chester and Pembroke, which, on the one hand, constituted the march of Wales, and, on the other, the still independent lordships of the north and west which made up *Pura Wallia* or Wales proper.

At the same time this political dualism can be allowed to loom too large in one's total view of the later Middle Ages in Wales. It is the novice grappling with the complexities of political narrative who makes the mistake of exaggerating the importance of this medieval political frontier. So widespread, in fact, was the survival into the thirteenth century of the cultural heritage of the pre-Norman age, even in those parts of the country which had fallen under the domination of Norman lords, that we shall be able in the sequel, as often as not, to lay aside (though not altogether discard) the bifocal lens, and so view in a common context much of what was happening during the age of the two Llywelyns over the greater part of Wales.

Norman cultural pressure, at least of a direct kind, was restricted, after all, to the valleys and lowlands of south Wales. The urban and manorial way of living had by 1200 barely touched the vast tracts of hill country in places such as

113

Glamorgan and Brecon. There, as in other lordships along the whole line of the eastern borderland, recaptured for Welsh speech and culture during the Welsh awakening of the twelfth century, marcher lords for long exercised but a loose and uncertain control over the native population, who, in outlook and mode of life, had more in common with the men of Gwynedd and Powys, Ceredigion and Ystrad Tywi, than with alien settlers and native bondmen of the southern lowlands.

Wales (irrespective of the distinction between the march and Wales proper) was still on the eve of the age of the Llywelyns predominantly a land of pastoral warrior tribesmen, largely dependent on servile labour, their isolated settlements lying far apart, separated by wide stretches of rough moorland and steep wooded valleys. The lives of the vast majority of Welshmen were dominated by local patriotism and intense family loyalties expressed in such things as the blood-feud and similar tribal customs. The physical barriers which kept families and clans apart also divided district from district, and this helped to perpetuate a highly morcellated political system with its numerous native and alien lords and mutually hostile states.

Now the belief is still far too common that this kind of life, which to all appearances shows very little advance on that which prevailed in Wales before the Normans came here, continued unchanged until after 1282 when final conquest by the English initiated certain forcible changes. There could be no greater error in interpreting the growth of the Welsh people.

Mountain folk may be notoriously conservative, reacting slowly and rather late in the day to new influences and ideas. But they are not unprogressive. As Sir Cyril Fox has so pertinently observed, a highland peasantry absorbs fresh ideas and adapts them to the native environment, so that in the end they emerge in what would often appear to be purely indigenous institutions. Part of the fascination of our present theme is to watch the older way of life undergoing a measure of radical transformation from the interaction of native institutions with ideas which were filtering through from the lower-lying peripheral areas of the march and from the wider world which lay beyond them.

The contrast between conditions in Wales and those which

existed in England where (at least in the lowlands beyond the
Welsh and Scottish marches) a much more advanced economy
and a considerable measure of strong central government had
grown up under the late Saxon and Norman kings, was not
lost on Welsh native leaders who, nearer home, had also ever
before them the example of efforts to organise more stable forms
of society in Norman settlements along the fringes of the march.
The great leaders of the twelfth century had played their part
in fostering similar trends in their territories, although the process was then so gradual that a contemporary observer like
Gerald was hardly aware of what was happening.

But between 1200, approximately, when Llywelyn the Great
rose to power in Gwynedd, and 1277, when Llywelyn's grandson, Llywelyn ap Gruffydd, faced tragic humiliation at the
hands of king Edward I, the forces to which I have been
referring in general terms, gathered rapidly increasing
momentum.

This is notably illustrated in the political and constitutional
policies of those two outstanding personalities. A proper
understanding of their main objectives must rest on a clear
realisation that the lordships of Wales proper had thus far
retained virtual independence, not merely because of strategic
considerations and temporary fluctuations in the fortunes of the
English monarchy, but also largely because of the good sense
of the leading rulers (whose example was followed by lesser
men) in acknowledging the overlordship of the king of England.
This principle had been finally asserted a generation before
Llywelyn the Great rose to power when such important figures
as Owain Gwynedd, the Lord Rhys, and Madog ap Maredudd
of Powys had sworn homage and fealty to king Henry II.

It was this feudalisation of the traditional superstructure of
Welsh politics, on the initiative of an alien power, which suggested to Llywelyn the Great the policy, carried out with
consummate skill during a long career of over forty years, of
securing so firm a mastery over his fellow lords in Powys,
Ceredigion and Ystrad Tywi, and other minor native lordships
in mid-Wales, as in effect (though never in his life-time an
accepted fact in law) to divert the allegiance of these lords
from the crown to himself. To facilitate the next step, namely

legal recognition of his authority by the crown (which incidentally was not secured until his grandson's time) the area of direct rule by the prince of Gwynedd himself was extended to cover the greater part of north Wales : and Llywelyn, in face of extreme opposition, schemed to perpetuate the power of his dynasty by uprooting the age-old custom of divided succession among the sons of a deceased ruler in favour of the feudal rule of succession by a single heir.

Thus his inheritance passed, in 1240, to David ap Llywelyn who rashly tried to force the issue by assuming the hitherto unknown title of prince of Wales. David died suddenly in 1246, at the height of hostilities launched by king Henry III with the avowed intention of destroying the achievements of Llywelyn's reign. His death postponed the hopes of that active minority of Welshmen who hoped to see Wales integrated into a genuine feudal state under the leadership of a single prince.

Some ten years later, however, the second Llywelyn (David's nephew and grandson of the great Llywelyn) taking full advantage of the domestic embarrassments of the English monarchy, reasserted the claims of his dynasty, again in face of much opposition from his own brothers and other lords of Wales. But from them all Llywelyn eventually exacted oaths of homage and fealty and then proceeded to assume the style *prince of Wales*. Even the most relentless of his domestic enemies, the anglophile lord of southern Powys, was forced to toe the line. Finally in the Treaty of Montgomery of 1267 (an important landmark in Welsh history) Henry III was obliged officially to acknowledge this *fait accompli*, reserving to himself the personal (and purely nominal) homage of the prince of Wales alone.

Thus with power extending from the outskirts of Carmarthen to the hinterland of Chester, and from Anglesey to the Brecon Beacons (for to Llywelyn had been conceded a considerable stake in the middle march including the marcher lordships of Builth and Brecon) the first, and indeed the only legally acknowledged, native prince of Wales entered on a brief ten year experiment in the control of a miniature feudal state.

Both and imaginative in conception, the policies of the two Llywelyns struck at the roots of the established order of things in Wales, flouted local sentiment and tribal feeling, and thus in the long run attracted the hostility of a fair proportion of Welshmen, although the princes were fortunate in having the fullest support of a number of far-sighted countrymen, among them some enlightened lawyers who had become familiar with the pattern of government in England.

It was with the aid of these lawyers that a stronger central authority now strove to extend its power to the social order as a whole. One of the most striking reflections of this trend is seen in those modifications of tribal customs which made the ordinary tribesmen more and more individually responsible for illegal acts to the prince and his subordinate lords. This revision of custom, moreover, resulted in revised codes of law which, though incorporating ideas borrowed from the common law of England, retained the traditional tone and form of earlier custom. There was thus produced one of the most notable monuments of early European jurisprudence — a *corpus* of customary law which continued to be associated with the name of Hywel Dda notwithstanding the fact that so many old practices were being entirely remodelled.

Again, although the economy of the highland zone of Wales continued to be predominantly pastoral, the free movement of the old warrior class had been giving way increasingly from about the middle of the twelfth century to more permanent and stable agricultural settlement ; and before the end of the period under review the land was dotted with small hamlets having some of the features of English villages, although the arable fields associated with these hamlets were organised on a peculiar communal basis adapted to the traditional tribal practices of the people. This medieval agrarian revolution, which reached its climax under the Llywelyns, pinpointed many of the sites of permanent rural occupation down to our own day ; fixed the spheres of tribal influence still preserved in modern parochial and township boundaries ; brought into existence new elements in the topographical nomenclature of the Welsh countryside ; in short, created the framework of an abiding landscape the details of which have been elaborated and recast in later generations.

By the third quarter of the thirteenth century, moreover, the natural, self-sufficient economy, characteristic of the Welsh uplands in the time of Gerald, had also been seriously undermined. Some trade and commerce, by sea and land, was drifting through from the boroughs of the anglicised parts of the march lands. A few towns and markets on the English model had been set up on the territories of the princes and their subordinate lords ; and the pressure of this growing money economy was already affecting fiscal practice there, and modifying social relationships in the rural hinterlands of the new native towns.

To meet these new trends, the princes reorganised local government, exploiting to the uttermost, in the interests of a well planned strategy, the economic resources of their dominions ; and then proceeded to introduce into the central government (itself a novel thing in Wales) all the trappings of English kingship under Welsh names. In their own small way the Llywelyns deserve to rank among the European state-builders of the thirteenth century, and they demonstrated in their achievements that all the preconditions of normal political growth existed in medieval Wales. But for the fact that the unfinished task of our last leader was cut short, Wales might well have developed along the same lines as Scotland with a Welsh Edinburgh — established perhaps at Abermule (in the country west of Shrewsbury) where Llywelyn ap Gruffydd might well have intended a Welsh capital to arise.

But this was not to be. The existence on England's western flank of a troublesome and increasingly powerful neighbour was intolerable to a king of England such as Edward I. The threat from the new Welsh principality was even more serious for the lords of the march of Wales, some of whom, notably the Mortimers and the Bohuns, had, by 1267, been driven out of their lands in the middle march. The most powerful of the marchers left *in situ*, the Clare lord of Glamorgan, had good reason to fear treachery from his own vassal chieftains in the hill country, and to suspect that the ambitions of Llywelyn ap Gruffydd included the hope of extending his power to the Severn sea.

By the close of the thirteenth century, it is true, many marcher lords must in some degree have assimilated part of the native

environment since in Wales they had for long played the role of
those Welsh rulers who had been unseated at the time of the
Norman conquest of the south, and had intermarried on a
broad front with ladies drawn from native ruling families.
Llywelyn the Great, for example, had not only himself married
a natural daughter of a king of England, but had arranged
alliances for his son, David, and four of his daughters with
members of marcher houses. (From one of those marriages,
incidentally, namely that between Gwladus Ddu and Ralph
Mortimer, is derived one of the two Welsh strains in Britain's
present royal line.)

Nevertheless, with their extensive interests and public re-
sponsibilities in England, the marchers were at heart as in-
imicable as the crown to the pretensions of native dynasties,
with whom marriage alliances were normally a matter of
political convenience at moments when the interests of both
parties were temporarily opposed to those of the crown. In
the end the implacable hostility of the marcher lords was a
factor of prime importance in the failure of Llywelyn ap
Gruffydd.

No less important, however, as a factor in Llywelyn's down-
fall was the unwilling co-operation of his subjects in the principality itself, not least of all among his own brothers and vassal
lords. The relentless pressure with which Llywelyn pursued
his domestic policies during the decade preceding the outbreak of the first Edwardian war in 1277, alienated many
ordinary Welshmen among churchmen and laymen alike. For,
despite the constitutional and social changes which have been
outlined, two generations were not enough to do more than
undermine, without as yet destroying, the visible form and
spirit of tribal society with its deep-seated regional loyalties.

A handful of poets, lawyers, and Cistercian monks might
share a broader vision of a Wales united in loyalty to a single
dynasty, but the spirit which still animated the majority of
Welshmen is illustrated when, at the close of the last struggle
for independence, Llywelyn's hapless brother, David, who
carried on the fight for a short time after Llywelyn's death,
was betrayed and handed over to the enemy (to quote a contemporary English writer) " by men of his own tongue."

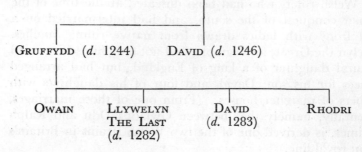

LLYWELYN THE GREAT (*d.* 1240)

GRUFFYDD (*d.* 1244)   DAVID (*d.* 1246)

OWAIN   LLYWELYN   DAVID   RHODRI
THE LAST   (*d.* 1283)
(*d.* 1282)

7. The Norman shell keep in the
grounds of Cardiff Castle

8. The Llywelyn ap Gruffydd Memorial
stone near Builth

THE CONQUEST OF WALES

By A. J Roderick

THE age of the two Llywelyns in the thirteenth century was one of the most dramatic periods in the history of Wales — a period of great triumphs for the house of Gwynedd, followed, quite suddenly, by complete disaster.

Gwynedd, in north-west Wales, was the most powerful of the independent Welsh lordships or principalities. And from 1255 to 1282 Llywelyn ap Gruffydd was its sole ruler. Before 1255 he and two of his brothers, Owen and David, had shared Gwynedd between them ; but in that year he dispossessed his brothers, and from then on he ruled alone. In dispossessing his brothers Llywelyn was not doing anything new. It was a commonplace of Welsh politics, and was indeed a political necessity for anyone who wished to build up a strong unified state. But Llywelyn's action won for him the lasting enmity of his brother David.

Llywelyn reached the peak of his career in the year 1267, with the Treaty of Montgomery. He was then acknowledged by the English king as Prince of Wales — a new title. This meant that the other independent Welsh rulers were now to acknowledge him as their overlord, to do homage and swear fealty to him, instead of to the English king as they had done in the past. That was a very important concession. Llywelyn also won for himself by this treaty extensive territories in the marches of Wales — lands which had been in English hands for generations. That was in 1267. Ten years later king Edward I of England made war on Llywelyn, and, in one campaign, deprived him of much of his territory and most of his power.

What had happened ? For one thing, the triumph of 1267 was founded not on a rock but on sand. There were several reasons for this. First of all, Llywelyn had been able to exploit the political situation in England, and he had done so with considerable skill. When the English barons (including many lords of the Welsh march) were in revolt against their king, Henry III, in the twelve-sixties, Llywelyn had supported them, because a weak monarchy in England suited him very well. But after 1267 that situation no longer existed. The Barons' War was over, and never again were political conditions in England to be so favourable for Llywelyn. Indeed, in 1272, when Henry III died, a king of very different calibre succeeded him — his son Edward I, one of the ablest and strongest monarchs ever to sit on the English throne.

Another factor unfavourable to Llywelyn was a direct result of his great success in 1267 ; because that success had been won at the expense of other people — the other Welsh princes, whose feudal superior he now was ; some of the marcher lords, men who had fought against their king, Henry III, but also men whose lands Llywelyn had overrun and was allowed to keep in 1267. These men were no longer against the crown ; they were now against Llywelyn. They wanted to recover their lost lands.

It is easy to point out in the twentieth century where Llywelyn went wrong in the thirteenth century. But go wrong he certainly did after 1267 ; that much is clear. What is not so clear is why he went wrong, why he behaved as he did in those critical years after the Treaty of Montgomery. His conduct aggravated the existing hostility against him. He antagonised the new king Edward I by refusing to pay the annual sums of money which he had bound himself by treaty to pay. He refused to perform the act of homage to Edward, although, again, bound by treaty to do so. He decided to marry Eleanor de Montfort. Eleanor was the daughter of Simon de Montfort, and Simon had been Llywelyn's ally and the leader of the baronial opposition against Henry III. Simon was now dead, but in wishing to marry his daughter did Llywelyn hope to revive the baronial struggle against the crown ? We do not know, but this proposed marriage certainly disturbed and annoyed Edward I. So much so that when Eleanor was sailing over from France to Wales in 1275, to marry Llywelyn, king Edward intercepted her ship in the Channel and took her prisoner.

Finally Llywelyn had enemies among his own fellow-countrymen. His younger brother David was already his enemy. Gruffydd ap Gwenwynwyn, ruler of southern Powys, was another enemy, and with David was plotting to assassinate Llywelyn.

By 1276 relations between Llywelyn and Edward were so bad that Edward and his council declared Llywelyn a rebel and decided on war.

Edward decided to launch a campaign against Llywelyn in north Wales in the summer of 1277, and to prepare the ground for that campaign during the preceding winter. This preliminary softening-up process was conducted from three centres, three royal castles, Chester, Montgomery and Carmarthen.

Its object was to destroy Llywelyn's power in the outlying areas of west Wales, mid-Wales, and north-east Wales, so as to shut him up in Gwynedd. This object was achieved and by the summer of 1277 all was ready for the main thrust against Llywelyn's citadel of Gwynedd, the mountains of Snowdonia and the plains of Anglesey.

Edward's plan of campaign was this. He was to advance from Chester along the coast by stages to the river Conway, while a fleet of ships was to land troops in Anglesey, thus penning Llywelyn in in the mountains.

The advance along the coast to the Conway estuary was not easy. The country was well wooded, suitable for the guerilla warfare at which the Welsh were expert. Edward's engineers built roads, cut down trees, and constructed castles. Flint and Rhuddlan marked the stages in the advance, and the final move was to Degannwy at the mouth of the river Conway. At all stages Edward had to protect his left flank from attack ; on his right was the sea. And across the Conway were the Welsh.

Meanwhile, Edward's seaborne force to Anglesey had landed there, and in August and early September had either destroyed or more probably confiscated the harvest of hay and crops. In west Wales the king's men had won control of the Towy valley and had crossed over into Ceredigion, making their way up to Aberystwyth.

Llywelyn was trapped. A winter campaign of attrition

lay ahead. And so he asked for terms. Edward, for his part, was quite willing to negotiate. It had been a costly campaign and he had no wish to prolong it. The result was the Treaty of Aberconway, 1277. It was a negotiated settlement, for Llywelyn had not surrendered unconditionally. But he was not in a strong position for bargaining, and the terms were severe.

Llywelyn was allowed to keep his title of prince of Wales, but he was no longer to be the overlord of the other independent Welsh rulers. The English king was now to be their overlord, as in the days before 1267. Llywelyn himself went to London at the end of the year, to do his long-delayed homage to king Edward. (The eighteenth century historian Carte, in his massive *History of England*, has an account of this visit, taken from an unpublished Mostyn manuscript) It is worth quoting : " The barons of Snowdon, with other noblemen of the most considerable families in Wales, had attended Llywelyn to London, when he came thither at Christmas, 1277, to do homage to Edward ; and, bringing, according to their usual custom, large retinues with them, were quartered in Islington and the neighbouring villages. These places did not afford milk enough for such numerous trains ; they liked neither wine, nor the ale of London, and were much displeased at a new manner of living . . . They were still more offended at the crowds of people that flocked about them when they stirred abroad, staring at them as if they had been monsters, and laughing at their uncouth garb and appearance : they were so enraged on this occasion that they engaged privately in an association to rebel at the first opportunity, and resolved to die in their own country rather than ever come again to London, as subjects, to be held in such derision."

So Llywelyn was stripped of his feudal authority over his fellow Welsh rulers. He was also stripped of territory. All the lands he had gained in 1267 he now lost. Anglesey was restored to him, but his eastern boundary now extended no further than the river Conway. All his mid-Wales territories he lost — Brecon, Builth, Gwerthrynion, Kerry, Cydewain, and most if not all of southern Powys.

The king's allies, David, Llywelyn's brother, and Gruffydd

ap Gwenwynwyn of southern Powys, were rewarded. David was given lands between the Conway and the Clwyd, and Gruffydd regained possession of southern Powys.

In 1278 king Edward released Eleanor de Montfort, and Llywelyn was allowed to marry her. The wedding took place in Worcester cathedral, with considerable pomp, the king and his queen being present. One imagines that the festivities must have seemed rather hollow to Llywelyn.

As a result of the war of 1277, not only did the marcher lords regain their lost territories, but the power of the crown in Wales was very much strengthened. In west Wales, Carmarthen and Cardigan had been royal castles for nearly fifty years, but the crown now had much more land there than formerly, including the castles of Dinefwr, Carreg Cennen, Llandovery and Aberystwyth, and the counties of Carmarthen and Cardigan were put in the charge of a new official, the Justice of West Wales, with his headquarters at Carmarthen. The lordship of Builth was back in royal hands, and in the north there were royal castles at Degannwy, Diserth and Rhuddlan, together with the coastal lands from Chester as far as the mouth of the river Conway. The crown was now, in effect, the biggest English landowner in Wales, with a host of royal officials to look after its interests.

The king's officials in the royal lands soon made themselves unpopular with the Welsh. They often carried out their duties with excessive zeal and with insufficient regard for the feelings of the people under their control, and this gave rise to a great deal of friction and resentment in many parts of Wales. There seems no doubt that Edward was, quite naturally, determined to prevent Llywelyn from recovering any of his former influence outside Gwynedd.

There were many disputes about land between Welshmen, marcher lords, and others, arising out of the war of 1277 and the Treaty of Aberconway ; and so Edward appointed seven judges to settle these disputes. The most important, and certainly the most delicate, case brought before the judges was a dispute between Llywelyn himself and his old enemy Gruffydd ap Gwenwynwyn of southern Powys. They both claimed the land of Arwystli — a sort of buffer territory between them.

Llywelyn wanted the dispute settled according to Welsh law, Gruffydd according to English law. The crown at first conceded Llywelyn's point, but the matter was an awkward one for Edward. If the case were to be tried by Welsh law, it was more than likely that the verdict would go to Llywelyn. And Edward was reluctant, understandably, to let his friend and ally Gruffydd ap Gwenwynwyn down. The proceedings were allowed — or perhaps encouraged — to drag on, and Edward began to insist that the case be tried according to English law. But before the dispute could be settled, the war of 1282 had broken out.

This war was fought to a finish. It was started, not by Edward, not by Llywelyn, although he had many grievances, but by Llywelyn's brother David. David had fought on the English side in 1277, and had been rewarded. He may have been dissatisfied about this. The lands he had been given lay adjacent to the royal lands in north Wales and we know that he himself and his people were smarting under the heavy-handed methods of the king's officials.

And so in March, 1282, David attacked and seized the castle of Hawarden, which was in English hands. This was not an impulsive act ; it had been carefully planned, and was followed immediately by similar attacks on English strongholds in north and west Wales and elsewhere. So far Llywelyn had had no part in this. But now circumstances forced his hand. He could not stand aside ; he was the national leader. He had to join in, whether he liked it or not.

King Edward made preparations for another Welsh war. His plan was much the same as in 1277 — an advance to the Conway river, a seaborne landing in Anglesey, and local campaigns in west and mid-Wales. The advance to the Conway was more difficult this time ; the opposition was more determined. The Anglesey force occupied the island, and then crossed the Menai Straits by means of a pontoon bridge to try and gain a footing on the mainland. But they were cut to pieces by Llywelyn's men.

Soon after this victory Llywelyn left David to look after Gwynedd, and with a body of troops made his way down to mid-Wales with the object of regaining lost ground there. There is some evidence that he was deliberately lured there by false promises of local support.

The events of the battle in which he was killed are not altogether clear, but this is the story as we have it. He reached a place called Llanganten, in the low hills two miles north-west of Builth, and there he halted. This was in December 1282. His immediate objective was probably the town and castle of Builth. But between him and Builth lay the river Irfon. There was a bridge across the river, and he sent a force down to take and hold that bridge.

Then he himself, with only one companion, left his headquarters to go to a pre-arranged rendezvous, to find out whether he could expect any co-operation from the local Welsh. Why he took such a risk with the English forces only a mile or so away is still a mystery.

While this was going on on the north side of the river, the English on the south side, in Builth, were not idle. Rather than sit still waiting for an assault, they decided to take the offensive. They discovered an undefended ford further along the river, and sent a party across it to attack the Welsh holding the bridge in the rear. The operation was a complete success. The men of Builth had executed that classic military manoeuvre known nowadays as a 'left hook.' The bridge was recaptured, and the main English force crossed over and made straight for the Welsh army on the rising ground north of the river.

Hearing the noise of battle, Llywelyn and his companion hastened back to his headquarters. But it was too late. They were seen, and some English horsemen gave chase. They overtook Llywelyn, and one of them, Stephen de Frankton, ran Llywelyn through with his lance and killed him, without knowing who he was. The Welsh army was defeated and put to flight. When Llywelyn's identity was discovered later that day, his head was cut off and sent to king Edward at Rhuddlan.

Llywelyn's wife Eleanor had died a few months earlier, in giving birth to her only child, a baby girl named Gwenllian. King Edward took charge of Gwenllian and sent her to an English nunnery.

The war went on for another six months after the death of Llywelyn. David took over the leadership, but his cause was now hopeless.   He was little more than a rebel on the run.   He was taken in June, 1283, tried, and put to death at Shrewsbury. The war was now over, and Welsh political independence was finally at an end.

THE SIGNIFICANCE OF 1284

By Glyn Roberts

In the long story of Wales, the fall of Llywelyn ap Gruffydd in 1282 is one of those historical turning points at which history really turned. An atmosphere of high tragedy surrounds the event, and it is well perhaps to remind ourselves of what actually happened in that year. The compiler of the chronicle called ' Brenhinedd y Saeson ' put it that " Wales was cast to the ground." In a quite literal sense, he over-simplified what had occurred. Despite his title, ' Prince of Wales', Llywelyn the Last had been no more than the lord of Gwynedd, with an uneasy right to the homage of the other Welsh lords ; and a very large part of Wales had long been in the hands of the crown and the marcher lords. Even after the death of Llywelyn, the lordship of Powys remained in the hands of its Welsh rulers as a marcher lordship. The death of Llywelyn marked the fall of a Welsh ruler whose conscious policy it had been to make himself and his principality a part of the feudal and political structure of the realm of England. And yet, the chronicler was essentially right in his view, for the year 1282 saw the end of the only practicable attempt ever made to solve the Welsh political problem.

Edward was determined to recognise no successor to Llywelyn, but the ways in which he tackled the question of what to do about Wales were determined by many factors which were beyond even his control. There could be no settlement which could apply to the whole territory of Wales, and certainly no unified system of government, law and administration to cover the whole country. The marcher lordships were still there after the fall of Llywelyn. Inevitably, therefore, the settlement carried out between 1282 and 1284 perpetuated that division which had been the outstanding feature of the Welsh political pattern throughout history, and

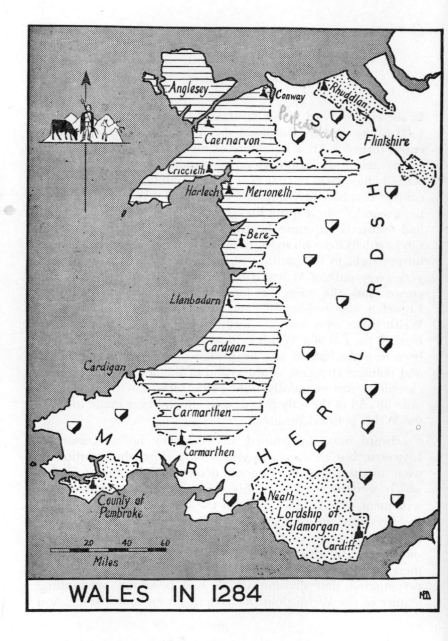

WALES IN 1284

which the princes of Gwynedd had worked so hard to overcome.

Long before 1282, the English crown had acquired territories in south Wales, and, in particular, royal lordships grouped around Carmarthen and Cardigan. These were, in effect, royal marcher lordships and they were governed and administered much as other marcher lordships. The king's authority was exercised through royal officials, administering a law which was an amalgam of English and Welsh elements. Edward was therefore left with the task of evolving a system of government only for those territories which he had wrested from Llywelyn in 1277 and 1284. But even in those areas he was not entirely free to do as he pleased. To reward those English barons who had helped him in his Welsh campaigns, he was obliged to create new independent lordships in the Perfeddwlad — Gwynedd to the east of the river Conway — and so there were established the new lordships of Denbigh, Ruthin, Chirk and Bromfield and Yale. He had a free hand therefore only in Gwynedd to the west of the Conway river — roughly Snowdonia and the isle of Anglesey — and in the small section of the Perfeddwlad which remained in his possession.

What he did in fact was to establish in these areas what might be called new royal lordships, somewhat on the model of his existing lordships in Carmarthen and Cardigan. By the ordinance of Rhuddlan, which he issued in March, 1284, Edward divided Snowdonia into the counties of Anglesey, Caernarfon and Merioneth, and these territories were placed under the authority of a new official, the Justice of North Wales, who had his administrative capital at Caernarfon. Out of the cantref of Englefield in the Perfeddwlad, he formed the county of Flint, which he placed under the rule of the Justice of Chester — an official who, of course, already existed. A Justice of South Wales, who governed the existing counties of Carmarthen and Cardigan, had been in office since 1280. There was thus no unity of structure in the government and administration even of the king's own dominions in Wales, apart from such attempts as the king might make to ensure uniformity of policy and practice amongst his officials. While Edward himself lived, the machinery which he had created was subject to a considerable degree of control ; but after his death in 1307 the tendency under weaker kings was for such central supervision to relax. The offices of Justice more and more became a baronial preserve, and not posts filled by royal servants in any strict sense of the term. In view of the increasing troubles of the crown during the fourteenth and fifteenth centuries, it would be difficult to argue convincingly that the quality of government in the royal possessions was substantially better than it was in the marcher lordships, which became proverbial for their lawlessness. To guard against further rebellion, Edward established in Gwynedd a great chain of castles — Caernarfon, Conway, Harlech, Cricieth and, later, Beaumaris — and in their shadows he planted boroughs inhabited by English immigrants who were encouraged to settle in them by grants of land and other privileges.

Each of the new shires was placed under a sheriff — yet another new officer — and a system of courts was set up on the pattern which was familiar to the king in England — the sessions, held by the justice, the county court, the sheriff's turn and the hundred or commote courts, presided over by the sheriff. The law which the courts were to administer combined the criminal law of England, and a civil law which was, in effect, a mixture of Welsh and English elements. It is almost needless to mention that it was the conscious policy of the crown to ensure that the highest offices in the new system were to be held by Englishmen — or more accurately, by non-Welshmen.

It is tempting at this stage to ask a whole series of questions. How far did the settlement of Gwynedd by Edward I involve a break with the past in that area ? What did the native Welsh think of it all, and how did they react to it ? Were the Welsh after 1284 a people struggling to recover their lost independence ? These are not easy questions to answer. It was not Edward's intention deliberately to alienate his new subjects, but the system he set up was harsh. Alien officials were unsympathetic and impatient of modes of life and thought with which they were not familiar. There were plentiful opportunities for officials to practise extortion and for evils of every kind to creep into the system. In the midst of a predominantly Welsh population were the English boroughs and the English

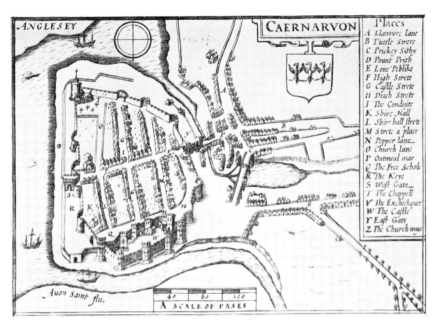

9. A 17th Century plan of Caernarvon town

10. Beaumaris Castle

burgesses, enjoying a monopoly of trade and commerce, and
providing an obvious focus of bitter racial conflict. These
things had long been known in royal and marcher lordships,
and now the people of Gwynedd were introduced to them.

And yet, the Welsh of Gwynedd must already have experienced some of the less attractive features of strong centralized
government as practised by those princes of Gwynedd who had
given the administration of their territories a " new look "
during the thirteenth century. A feudalised criminal law was
not a new thing in Gwynedd in 1284, and the felon who was
hanged under modified Welsh law by Llywelyn's officials probably felt as badly about it as did his felonious successor who
was condemned at the new justice's sessions. The absence of
Welsh judicial and administrative records for the period before
1282 makes impossible any precise estimate of the ways in
which the incidents of strong government pressed upon the
prince's subjects. But there can be no doubt that the shoe had
pinched. There is some evidence to show that Llywelyn the
Last's subjects knew what it was to suffer from the extortion
of their prince. The concept that the administration of justice
was a source of profit, and the efficient, indeed, over-efficient
insistence on royal rights in the matter of finance and taxation,
were no new experiences to the Welsh of Gwynedd in 1284.

Again, Edward's task in dealing with Llywelyn's ambitions
had been eased by the fact that not all Welshmen approved of
them. The Welsh lords of Powys and Deheubarth had no love
for his masterful policy and they had sided very firmly with
Edward I in the final struggles. Within Gwynedd itself,
Llywelyn had been at bitter odds with the Church, or at least,
with the bishops of Bangor and St. Asaph. More striking is
one strange and brief entry in the *Peniarth 20* version of the
Chronicle of the Welsh Princes. After describing the opening
of the fateful war of 1282 and Edward's conquest of Anglesey,
the chronicler goes on to say this : " and then was effected the
betrayal of Llywelyn, in the belfry at Bangor, by his own men."
There is no direct available evidence to explain the entry, but
it has about it a precision which suggests that it was well
founded. It is worth noting, for example, that many of
Llywelyn's councillors and officials retained their privileges,

and much of their importance, in the period following his
death ; and it can be shown that many prominent Welshmen
in Gwynedd took advantage of the proclamation issued by
Edward I during his last campaign, promising security in their
rights and privileges to those who were prepared to submit to
him. Amongst them, for example, was a number of the
descendants of Ednyfed Fychan, seneschal in his day to
Llywelyn the Great ; up to the eve of the final conquest some
of his sons and grandsons had continued to hold high office
under the prince of Gwynedd. But at least two members of
this great family actually served in Edward's armies in the
campaign of 1282.

All this points to the conclusion that there were many
Welshmen, within Gwynedd and without, who were not sorry
to see the end of Llywelyn ; and as they were men of the world
and men of affairs, they presumably knew what they were
doing, and what the alternative to Llywelyn was likely to be.
The existence of political realists of this type is not surprising
when we remember the historical background out of which
they grew. About a century earlier Gerald the Welshman had
made the point that the Welsh had learnt the use of arms and
the management of horses from the Normans and the English,
" with whom," he said, " they had much intercourse." But
they learnt other things, too. The official class which had
been created by the vigorous policy of Gwynedd — military
leaders, lawyers, administrators and diplomats — had close
and intimate contacts with English barons and the English
court. Like Llywelyn himself, they had become part of a
pattern which was much broader in extent than Wales, and
their horizons were not always limited by purely Welsh considerations. Nothing is more striking than the rise in Gwynedd
and Deheubarth during the reigns of Edward I and Edward II
of a Welsh official class whose members threw themselves whole-
heartedly into the administrative and other tasks which were
given to them. Its leaders were of the house of Ednyfed
Fychan. One branch of this clan provided the Welsh ancestors
of the later royal Tudors, and throughout the fourteenth
century this particular family was regularly and closely connected with the royal service. It may well be that the early

Tudors, descended from a family of royal officials in Gwynedd, found it easy to transfer their services to new masters. The practice introduced by Edward I of granting to the king's eldest son the title and revenues of the Prince of Wales probably helped the transition.

The descendants of Ednyfed were not the only Welsh *uchelwyr* to follow the same line. It was not unusual for the office of sheriff — and particularly the office of deputy sheriff — to be given to Welshmen of full blood, and the office of *rhaglaw* in the commotes was usually held by Welshmen. When Gruffydd ap Adda of Ynysmaengwyn in Merioneth died sometime after 1344, the only fact recorded by his relatives on his tombstone, apart from his name, was that he had held the office of *Rhaglaw* of the commote of Ystumanner in 1331 and 1334. The inscription can be seen in Towyn church to this day. As we come to know more about the early history of individual Welsh *uchelwr* families, it becomes increasingly clear that the more successful of them associated themselves regularly with the administrative system, both under the crown and under marcher lords. It is true that men of this type sometimes found cause to regret the line they had chosen ; such leaders of rebellion as Rhys ap Maredudd in 1287 and Madog ap Llywelyn in 1294 were men who did not like the new world in which they found themselves, although they had done their best to bring it into being. But in general these co-operators with the new system were ready to continue their association with it, and with political leaders and factions in England. The fruit of their labours is to be seen at its most obvious in such phenomena as the rise of the great houses of Herbert and Dynevor in the fifteenth century, and less obviously in that silent process whereby the *uchelwyr* of Gwynedd gained practical control of the machinery of government in the Principality of North Wales by the opening of the Tudor period.

In view of these trends, it is not surprising that the " court poetry " of the fourteenth century, written mainly in praise of the *uchelwyr*, reveals little trace of anti-English feeling. Indeed, the greatest of all the fourteenth century poets — Dafydd ap Gwilym — was himself a member of a family which for generations had been closely connected with the royal service in

Wales. His contemporary, Iolo Goch, sang not only to Roger Mortimer, earl of March, the greatest of all the marcher lords — after all, the Mortimers were his landlords — but also to Edward III, who, of all English kings up to the close of the fourteenth century, has perhaps the poorest claim to be regarded as a Welsh benefactor. Admittedly, there is a type of Welsh poetry in the Middle Ages which gives a very different impression. Ever since the ninth century at least, another class of bards had been producing a mass of dark, obscure prophetic poetry. Its general theme was the expectation that a deliverer would one day appear to avenge the Welsh on their Saxon oppressors. While it may well reflect a genuine layer of feeling and opinion, it may also represent a popular literary fashion only. Certainly, it is difficult to connect it in any way with the known attitudes of the *uchelwr* class in the fourteenth century. One is sometimes tempted to think that this type of poetry reflects only that attitude of mind which today finds pleasure and satisfaction in Old Moore's Almanac and the weekly astrologer's column in the popular press. In the fifteenth century its conventions were to be harnessed to the purposes of propaganda during the Wars of the Roses.

All this does not mean, of course, that Wales was consumed with enthusiasm for the Edwardian settlement, or for the system of marcher lordships. At best their methods were stern and harsh, as all methods of government tended to be in the Middle Ages ; at worst, they were tyrannical and corrupt, and the worst tended to become the normal condition as the Middle Ages drew to their uneasy and lawless conclusion. Of course, there were in Welsh society those ordinary people who were far removed from those classes — English and Welsh — who profited from government and administration. We do not know what they felt. In any case, new forces were at work during the fourteenth century — social and economic changes which set up new stresses and strains in the social pattern. There were the changes which helped to create the background to the great revolt of Owain Glyn Dŵr at the close of the century, with its strong anti-English flavour. Racial hatred was always potentially present in medieval Wales. In a period of change and confusion, it was very easy for Welshmen to assume that their sufferings were caused by English dominance from without and by English settlements and officialdom from within.

THE PROSE ROMANCES OF MEDIEVAL
WALES

By Gwyn Jones

THERE are so many meanings attached to the word Romance, even in the field of literature, and even with a capital R, that I had better start by explaining that, for my purpose, a prose romance is any continuous narrative in prose.   Simpler still, a prose story.   It follows that my real business is with the Mabinogion.

Still, it is proper to notice that Wales had other medieval romances besides the contents of the Mabinogion.   Thus, if we accept the famous, though rather inadequate, medieval classification of story as the Matter of Britain, the Matter of France, and the Matter of Rome the Great, we shall find all three represented, however thinly, in Welsh literature. Stories about Arthur, the Matter of Britain, about Charlemagne, the Matter of France, and the wide-ranging collection of classical and not so classical subjects that comprised the Matter of Rome — these were for the most part international currency in western and northern Europe for many centuries.   They were written about in many languages, but the stuff itself was very much the same.   If you were born any time during the thirteenth century, could read, and lay your hands on manuscripts, you could keep yourself remarkably well informed about the Holy Grail, Charlemagne's Pilgrimage, and the Exploits of Alexander the Great, whether you were born in Bavaria, Burgundy, Bologna, Bornholm in the Baltic, or Brecon in Wales.   Now most of our Welsh examples of this kind of literature, as you would expect, are translations or adaptations of French books ;   though just one or two, like the Seint Greal and our version of the Seven Sages of Rome, show some power to vary the pattern.   But no literature was ever great by imitation alone, and it is simple truth that if works like these were all that medieval Welsh prose

138

literature had to offer, that literature would be a very small paragraph in the literary history of western Europe. So, as I began by saying, our business is with the Mabinogion. For it is there we shall find Wales's own distinctive contribution to medieval prose literature.

The word Mabinogion, as we all know, was the title given to her translations from the Red Book of Hergest by Lady Charlotte Guest. Between them, the Red Book and the White Book of Rhydderch, which was written down about 1300–1325 (some 75 years before the Red Book), have preserved for us eleven prose stories.

These stories fall quite naturally into three easily distinguished and yet inter-related groups. First there are the Four Branches of the Mabinogi : *Pwyll Price of Dyfed*, *Branwen Daughter of Llŷr*, *Manawydan Son of Llŷr*, and *Math son of Mathonwy*. Second come four native Welsh tales, independent of the Four Branches on the one hand, and of the romances proper on the other. Two of these are short folk-tales, *The Dream of Macsen Wledig* and *The Adventure of Lludd and Llefelys*. The other two, *Culhwch and Olwen* and *The Dream of Rhonabwy*, have much to tell of Arthur and his warriors ; but even so their Welsh provenance sets them emphatically apart from the three so-called 'French' Arthurian romances of the third group ; *The Lady of the Fountain*, *Peredur son of Efrawg* and *Gereint Son of Erbin*.

For a start, is there anything to be said by way of generalisation about the substance of these eleven tales ? From the very fact that they are divisible into clearly marked groups, we shall expect them to show marked differences. And the differences are indeed considerable, in matter and manner, in atmosphere and age. They range from the primitive to the courtly, from the heroic to the romantic ; the charming to the terrible, the fantastic to the matter-of-fact, from comedy to tragedy, the pathetic to the sublime ; from a brutal simplicity to a strained sophistication. We think of the Mabinogion as a book, but we should do as well to think of it as a library. It is every bit as much the one as the other.

And yet the stories are bound together by something more than their preservation in the same manuscript. For one thing they are all Welsh. *Branwen Daughter of Llŷr* uses a lot of Irish material, but it is not Irish. *The Lady of the Fountain* stands in some relationship or other to Chrêtien de Troyes, but it is not French. They are both Welsh, and I think that is worth insisting on. Then second, for all their variety they belong unmistakably to one literary and social setting. And third, there is a strong connecting thread in their subject matter, which is tradition, though it is certainly not historical tradition. True, in the Four Branches there is mention of Taliesin, the sixth-century poet, and Caswallon, who was known to Julius Caesar as Cassivellaunus. Mascen in the story which bears his name was the Spanish-born Magnus Maximus who invaded Gaul in the year 383 and was killed at Aquileia five years later; and the hero of one of the romances is Owein son of Urien, a famed prince of the North Britons in the late sixth century. There is even Arthur himself. But in the Mabinogion these characters do not play their historical role. They are by this time heroic figures from a misty past about whom has gathered the folk literature of the early Welsh. For the subject matter of the Mabinogion, from which the separate stories are derived, is first and foremost mythology in decline, and folktale, blended with such explanatory stories as are beloved of all the world's people, tales to account for place names or the names of persons, tales to explain customs or proverbs. This can be seen most clearly in the Four Branches and Culhwch, but to the discerning eye it is pervasive of the romances too.

But you may well be asking : how was this ancient material kept alive till the time of the manuscripts, or rather till the time it was written down in the form in which we have it ? And why did it undergo such extensive changes ? Well, it was kept alive, and likewise altered, by the people whose business it was to know and relate such stories; the story-tellers, or *cyfarwyddau*, the classic mention of whom is to be found in the story of *Math*. When Gwydion and his eleven companions set off for Rhuddlan Teifi, to trick Pryderi, they travelled in the guise of bards. ' " Why," said Pryderi, " gladly would we have a tale from some of the young men yonder." " Lord," said Gwydion, " it is a custom with us that the first night after one comes to a great man, the chief bard shall have the say. I will tell a tale gladly." Gwydion was the best teller of tales in the world. And that night he entertained the court with pleasant tales and story-telling till he was praised by everyone in the court, and it was pleasure for Pryderi to converse with him.'

In the memories of a thousand Gwydions, during many hundreds of years, a great wealth of story was endlessly adapted to its narrator's purpose. They preserved, added, rejected, explained or forgot, until eventually we are dealing with men whom we must call authors in our modern sense. We do not know their names, but someone was responsible for the Four Branches in the second half of the eleventh century, and some-one for the *Dream of Rhonabwy* about a hundred years later. And so with the other stories of the White Book and the Red.

So much, then, by way of general consideration. And now to come to closer quarters with the question : Why is the Mabinogion important ? Why do we prize it so highly com-pared, say, with those other Welsh medieval prose narratives which you may feel I disposed of in little time and with little enthusiasm ? The answer ought to be a very long one, but I am afraid I shall have to make it short. In brief then, because the Mabinogion is great literature.

I hope you will agree that no other answer would carry much weight. I might have said, and all these things would be true, that the Mabinogion is important for its folklore, as a demon-stration of how stories were transmitted in the Middle Ages, as a repository of Celtic tradition, as an assemblage of comparative literary material, or even as a collection of interesting stories. But where does that take us ? For when the palaeographer and philologist, the student of folklore and religion, even the literary historian, have had their say, what really matters is the Mabinogion's value as a work of art.

Now time alone compels me to dispose of two-thirds of these stories in very cursory fashion. I am not going to talk at all about *Lludd and Llefelys*, which is a nice little folk tale. I am not even going to talk about *Macsen*, though it is a great favourite of mine, and a lovely golden bowl of a story. I am not going to talk about the *Dream of Rhonabwy*, like *Macsen* the work of a quite brilliant author, enamelled with words like some lovely illuminated manuscript with colours, and unique in its blended appreciation and mockery of Arthur and the great men of the past. And finally I am not going to say anything — much

— about what we can in the strictest sense of the words call the three Arthurian romances.

Just this much perhaps — that of their kind they are very good indeed. They are not too long, are quite well planned, and in their execution remarkably tidy. They all three contain episodes and narrative strokes in the best tradition of Welsh story-telling : the silver bowl, the thunder and the deadly shower, in *The Lady of the Fountain*, or the opening section of *Peredur*, or in the third romance the hedge of mist, the apple tree, and the horn which Gereint blew. They are unlocalised, I agree, their Arthur is the shadow of a shade, and their heroines pallid ; nor are their emotional colouring and social and moral code likely to set the bells ringing for us today. But if we judge them as medieval romances — and it is pointless to judge them as anything else — then I must say I read them each time with increased respect for the skill and tact of their authors. Finally, they are an important part of the Matter of Britain, the story of Arthur, as it is recorded in Welsh medieval prose literature.

These six stories disposed of — and I shudder at the brutality of the disposal — we are left with the Four Branches of the Mabinogi and *Culhwch and Olwen*, and I think that here, along with the *Dream of Macsen Wledig*, the Mabinogion ceases to be good literature and rises to greatness.

The Four Branches first. The Four Branches of the Mabinogi means the four parts of the story, and in so far as we have anyone's story here, it is that of Pryderi. He is conceived and born, and reared to boyhood in the First Branch. He survives the fatal expedition to Ireland in the Second. He is rapt away to the Otherworld, and then restored to earth, in the Third ; and in the Fourth Branch he is killed by our friend the story-teller, magician and shape-shifter, Gwydion son of Dôn. But this is not even the skeleton of the Four Branches. In the Second Branch, that of *Branwen Daughter of Llŷr*, Pryderi receives only a bare mention ; the author is concerned with a quite different story, that of Branwen herself, and into this story he has incorporated a great bulk of Irish rather than Welsh tradition. In the Fourth Branch, that of *Math*, his death is incidental to the story of Lleu Llaw Gyffes, and how he was betrayed by Gronw Bebyr, who was killed for it, and his wife Blodeuedd, who was turned into an owl for it.

Confronted with this almost painful simplification of the substance of the Four Branches, we may well expect the question : Why then rate the Four Branches so highly ? In them we have a broken design and mutilated fragments, great confusions and unanswerable problems. And yet, we say, a masterpiece. Why ?

The first requisite of great literature is that it shall be greatly written. The Four Branches are so written, by an incomparable master of expression, who wrote Welsh in harmony with the purest genius of the language. That in itself is an artistic miracle. Second, he told superb stories, and told them not only in perfect language, but with superb art. The problems scholars find in *Hamlet* have not prevented it from being one of the world's best plays. The problems of the Four Branches are no more serious. And like *Hamlet*, the Four Branches are more than the sum of their parts : they are, in addition to everything else, a commentary on existence. *Branwen*, in particular, when it recounts Brân's journey to Ireland, the last great battle, the death of Branwen, and the Assembly of the Wondrous Head, gives us that effect of revelation and extension of time and place which lies beyond the reach of all save the world's greatest writers. Our author's range is wide, and his touch certain. In narration and dialogue he shows the same control, and there is a high nobility about his work even when it deals with ignoble but all too human failings. And he has the final mark of a writer of the first class : the greater his material, the more greatly he handles it.

The author of *Culhwch and Olwen* is of quite another turn. He has quite another story, and is doing something entirely distinctive with it. His tale is at once simple and complex. So simple that its substance may be indicated in a sentence ; so complex that its ramifications could hardly be followed in an hour. In essence it is the far-spread folktale of the Winning of the Giant's Daughter. It is Culhwch's destiny set on him by his stepmother, that he shall marry none save Olwen daughter of Yspaddaden Chief Giant. With Arthur's aid he finds his bride, accomplishes the tasks the Giant sets him, and marries her — and when the Giant's daughter gets married, as we all know, the Giant must die. The tasks Culhwch and his helpers must discharge include some of the oldest folk-themes in literature : the Freeing of the Prisoner, the Helping Companions, the Oldest Animals, the lame Ant, and the Hunting of the Otherworld Boar.

There are, I think, three main reasons why *Culhwch and Olwen* is second only to the Four Branches as a Welsh medieval prose romance.

In the first place, it is a treasure-house of the lore of early Britain. Sometimes we have no knowledge of the persons and events it refers to ; they have been swallowed up in a night of oblivion. Sometimes we have a glimmering knowledge only, from Welsh or Irish, or more widely from comparative folklore and religion. But here they are, by the score ; and this alone would make *Culhwch and Olwen* a very important work.

Second, it occupies a unique position among Arthurian prose romances. For Culhwch's Arthur is not the idealised, and devitalised, monarch of European romance ; nor is he quasi-historical as in Nennius ; but the beneficent folk-hero, the fabulous barbaric chieftain of a barbarous fantastic court, a tremendous man of action, a killer of monsters. In other words, he is the British Arthur. The document which so amply tells of him is therefore of high importance.

Then, third, and most important, this story is a supreme achievement of its kind, written by a man of manifold powers, and an exultant, virtuoso's joy in their employment. He is a highly self-conscious author always exploring the possibilities of language. Brutal curtness, a tender lyricism, the gravely beautiful or the headlong gasconade — he is endlessly resourceful and endlessly exciting. And he has a matchless yarn to tell.

So there we are. The Four Branches, Culhwch, the other native tales, and the three romances. The Mabinogion. This was our real contribution to medieval prose romance. We may well be proud of those unknown story-tellers and authors who left us this impressive monument of our Welsh past.

GEOFFREY OF MONMOUTH AND THE
'MATTER OF BRITAIN'

By A. O H. Jarman

HITHERTO we have been dealing with the development of Wales within her own borders from the earliest times to the Middle Ages. We are now concerned with something rather different, with what may perhaps be called the cultural expansion of Wales. For during the twelfth and thirteenth centuries, while the Welsh princes were endeavouring to build an enduring political structure in the face of continued Norman and English aggression, Wales suddenly found herself wielding an immense influence outside her own territory in a totally different sphere, that of imaginative literature. In a comparatively short space of time Welsh tradition made a contribution of the first importance both to the content and to the orientation of European literature, and when we speak of the ' Matter of Britain ' it is to that contribution that we refer. Strictly speaking the ' Matter of Britain,' the *Matière de Bretagne,* was a theme or series of themes in medieval French literature, in which it occupied a place alongside the ' Matter of France ' and the ' Matter of Rome.' It meant, in short, the Arthurian Legend, the whole vast complex of tradition and story concerning the court of king Arthur which provided French and several other literatures with such a considerable part of their subject-matter during the later Middle Ages.

Of Arthur as a historical person nothing is known with any degree of certainty. Scholars, however, are willing to believe that such a person may have existed, and probably did exist, towards the end of the fifth or the beginning of the sixth century. He seems to have been a military figure rather than a king, a general leading the Britons in their struggle against the Anglo-Saxons. There are no contemporary references to him, but traditions concerning him are preserved in the *Historia Brittonum,* or ' History of the Britons ', compiled by Nennius early in the ninth century. There it is stated that Arthur was victorious over his enemies in twelve battles and that in the final and decisive battle of the Badonic Hill he struck down nine hundred and sixty of the opposing army with his own hand. There are references to him also in several Welsh poems of the early Middle Ages, and in the well-known prose tale *Kulhwch ac Olwen,* believed to date from about 1100, Arthur and his men play a leading part. Here, however, the milieu is that of folklore, and Arthur and his followers live in a marvellous world of superhuman beings, giants, witches, monsters and talking animals. Arthur's court is in Cornwall and his horizons hardly extend beyond south-western England, south Wales and Ireland.

During the twelfth century all this was changed. In a few decades Arthur was transformed into a great European monarch, a feudal emperor whose court was frequented only by the fairest ladies and the boldest and most chivalrous knights. The setting of primitive folklore was replaced by the refinement and sophistication of medieval romance. No one person can be credited with having brought about the whole of this change, but the foremost influence at work was the new conception of Arthur presented to the international literary world by Geoffrey of Monmouth.

Of Geoffrey himself not very much is known. He is believed to have been a member of a family of Bretons who had come over during or after the Norman Conquest and settled in Monmouth. After many years spent as a secular canon at Oxford he was ordained priest and consecrated bishop of St. Asaph in 1152. Since, however, St. Asaph was in Welsh hands and Geoffrey was a Norman nominee he did not visit his diocese. The work on which his fame rests is the *Historia Regum Britanniae,* ' The History of the Kings of Britain', first published in 1136, and purporting to be an account of the history of the Britons from the time of Brutus, who was supposed to have flourished about eleven hundred years before Christ, to that of the better-authenticated Cadwaladr in the seventh century of our era.

In his preamble Geoffrey disclaims all originality and affirms that his work is merely a translation into Latin of ' a certain very old book in the British tongue ' which had been brought to his notice by Walter, archdeacon of Oxford. Now, although Walter was a real person, contemporary with Geoffrey and without doubt known to him personally, this statement is not now generally believed to be true. Geoffrey was a great imaginative writer and in ascribing all his varied and colourful material to an ancient chronicler in the British tongue, whether Welsh or Breton, he was doing himself very much less than justice. On the other hand, he did of course use many sources, and much research has gone into trying to discover what they were. Nennius' *Historia Brittonum* was certainly one, and he may have used other sources of a Welsh character which are not now known to us. He used material from foreign sources as well, biblical, classical, and medieval, but nevertheless the broad conception of the work, its spirit, its majestic sweep, are Geoffrey's and Geoffrey's alone and constitute his title to literary fame.

There has in recent years been much speculation concerning Geoffrey's motive in writing the *Historia*. No doubt there is some truth in the view that above all else he was one who enjoyed telling a good story. It must not be forgotten, however, that he was a Breton dependent on Norman favour and offering a Norman audience a highly-coloured account of the ancient glories of the Welsh people who were at that very time resisting Norman aggression with arms.

Now it is obvious that Geoffrey was fully conscious of the fact that the Bretons and the Welsh were originally the same people. His book is a panegyric on his own race in the far distant past. He gives the Brythonic peoples a classical descent from Brutus the Trojan, whom he thought of as a sort of Greek, and then fills the thousand years to the time of Caesar with a long line of illustrious but imaginary reigns and monarchs. When he arrives at the Roman period his writing of history becomes a little more circumspect. Pure invention would not do here. The Roman conquest is admitted but nevertheless the impression conveyed that Roman authority in Britain was hardly more than nominal. The Brythonic settlement of Brittany is put towards the end of the Roman period and here Geoffrey makes it quite clear that in his view those who migrated were the best and most virile elements among the Britons. For the inferior remnant left behind there was now no choice but to seek protection from Rome against their enemies, and on more than one occasion also they received the help of their Breton cousins. It was in fact only during the reign of Arthur that the insular Britons for a time regained their former honour and renown, and even Arthur was largely dependent on Breton support. After the close of Arthur's reign an inglorious century and a half ensued, ending with the death of Cadwaladr, last of the ancient kings of the Britons, at which point Geoffrey breaks off his narrative.

There was therefore little likelihood of the Normans' gaining the impression that Geoffrey was pro-Welsh in the contemporary political sense. Rather would they feel satisfaction and pride at the thought that they were the inheritors by conquest of a land possessing such long and splendid martial traditions.

On the Welsh, however, the impact of Geoffrey's book was rather different. It was well received in Wales and before the end of the twelfth century was translated into Welsh by at least three different translators. For many centuries the *Brut y Brenhinedd*, as the *Historia* was called, continued to enjoy enormous prestige. After the loss of independence, in particular, the contemplation of a resplendent past, so unexpectedly revealed by Geoffrey's glowing narrative, served in some measure to compensate for the sense of national degradation. Political poets in the fourteenth and fifteenth centuries sought to awaken the ardour of their fellow-countrymen by referring to the exploits of their ancestors, as described by Geoffrey, and Renaissance scholars like Sir John Prys and Humphrey Lhuyd devoted much time and effort to vindicating the genuineness of the ' British History', as it was then called. By that time Geoffrey's work was beginning to feel the blast of modern criticism, but even in the eighteenth century a Welsh prose classic, Theophilus Evans' *Drych y Prif Oesoedd*, was largely inspired by the *Historia*, and for many years Lewis Morris laboured to uphold Geoffrey's claim that his work was a translation of an ancient book written in the British tongue.

The Arthurian part of the *Historia* occupies about a fifth of the entire work. It is here, for the first time in literary history, that Arthur is portrayed as a great conqueror. Ascending the throne at the age of fifteen, he begins his career by driving the pagan English out of Britain. Then the Picts of Scotland, the Scots of Ireland and the inhabitants of the Northern Isles and Scandinavia are subdued. France is next invaded and the whole country surrenders after a tremendous single combat between Arthur and Frollo, the French king. Arthur is then crowned amid scenes of great splendour at Caerleon or Caer-llion-ar-Wysg. As a native of Gwent, Geoffrey was no doubt familiar with the remains of the Roman town and camp at Caerleon, still not completely obliterated in the twelfth century. Quite understandably it was here, rather than in Cornwall, that he decided to place Arthur's court and he gives us a lyrical description of the City of the Legions, situated on the noble river Usk, surrounded by woods and meadows, and in the magnificence of its buildings comparable to Rome herself. It was to Caerleon that the challenge of the Roman emperor Lucius was sent, bidding Arthur either submit to him or prepare for war. Submission was out of the question and Arthur and his hosts again made for the Continent. It was veritably a war between east and west. Against Arthur and his allies were ranged not only the Roman emperor but also the kings of Greece, Parthia, Lybia, Egypt, Babylon and many other countries. After much fighting the emperor was defeated but, while Arthur was crossing the Alps on his way to Rome, news came that Medrawd, or Modred, his sister's son, had betrayed him at home and usurped his throne. He returned immediately and both he and Medrawd fell in the general slaughter at Camlan. Geoffrey brings the story to an end rather equivocally with the statement that Arthur, though mortally wounded, was borne away to the island of Afallon — *in insulam Auallonis* — to be healed of his wounds. One of the translators of the *Historia* into Welsh adds a sentence here expressing surprise at the ambiguity of this statement. There is no doubt that a belief existed at this time among the Welsh, and also the Cornish and the Bretons, that Arthur was to return to lead them to ultimate victory over their enemies. Geoffrey's words are a veiled reference to this belief. To have declared it more explicitly would have been an indiscretion.

The publication of Geoffrey's version of British history caused both excitement and astonishment among twelfth century historians. Here was an account of the early Britons, their kings, wars and conquests, almost completely at variance with what was generally believed to be historical fact. For centuries, however, few ventured to challenge it. In the twelfth century itself only one historian, William of Newburgh, attacked it openly, declaring it to be a collection of fairy-tales. Gerald of Wales also expressed his disapproval in characteristic fashion at the end of a lengthy account of the afflictions of a certain Meilyr, an inhabitant of Caerleon, who was troubled by devils, especially those concerned with the propagation of untruth. On one occasion, says Gerald, the Gospel of St. John was placed on the man's bosom, whereupon the devils immediately vanished, but when, merely as an experiment, Geoffrey's *Historia* was substituted for it, they returned in even greater numbers and caused more distress than before. Such opinions, however, were exceptional. Strange as it may seem, Geoffrey's version of history was accepted and generally regarded as authoritative until the close of the Middle Ages.

In the sphere of imaginative literature Geoffrey's influence was even wider. It is in his *Historia*, for instance, that the story of Lear and his daughters was first told. This, and the portrayal of Arthur, are Geoffrey's principal contribution to the content of European literature. It is of course true that the *Historia* was not the only channel for the transmission of Arthurian material, but for the conception of Arthur as a mighty emperor whose court was the centre of the world Geoffrey alone was responsible.

The popularization of his work began in earnest in 1155, when a poem of some 15,000 lines, the *Roman de Brut*, was completed by Wace, a native of Jersey. Written in Norman-French, it sought to make the material of the *Historia* accessible to a wider public who knew no Latin. It did contain some additional matter, however, and it is in this poem that we hear for the first time of the Round Table, designed to maintain absolute equality between Arthur's knights. About half a century later the whole story was told in Middle English, in a poem of some 32,000 lines by Layamon, the most considerable

English poet of the period. These works, however, are not Arthurian romances in the full sense. They occupy an intermediate position between Geoffrey's *Historia*, written in chronicle form and offered to the public as history, and the great collection of French prose tales, written about the beginning of the thirteenth century and known as the Vulgate Cycle of Romances.

This group of tales comprises five lengthy texts : (1) *The History of the Holy Grail* ; (2) *The Story of Merlin* ; (3) *The Story of Lancelot* ; (4) *The Quest of the Holy Grail* ; and (5) *The Death of Arthur*. The Grail stories were a typically French development of the Arthurian theme, and the *Lancelot* portrays its hero in countless adventures as the exemplar of chivalry. It is the other two tales, the *Merlin* and the *Death of Arthur* (*Mort Artu*), that stem largely from the *Historia*. In the first of these Geoffrey's portrait of Merlin, the magician who brought about the conception of Arthur by Uthr Pendragon, originally the Myrddin of Welsh tradition, is elaborately developed. A famous incident is Merlin's final encounter with Viviane, who had persuaded him to impart some of his secrets to her and was thus enabled to imprison him for ever in a tower of enchantment in the forest of Brocéliande. The *Mort Artu* tells of the treachery of Mordred, the fall of Arthur and his translation to Avalon. Although many additions are made to the narrative, these incidents, the most celebrated in the whole Arthurian story, are derived from Geoffrey's *Historia* and from his only other known work, the *Vita Merlini* or ' Life of Merlin', a highly fanciful poem of over 1500 lines, composed some twelve years after the *Historia*. It was in this poem that Geoffrey referred to the ' island of apples known as the Fortunate Isle', and wrote the first description in literature of Arthur's voyage to the Celtic Otherworld. There the wounded king was laid on a golden bed and told that if he remained long enough he could be healed of his wound. Whether or not he would be healed, however, was uncertain, and Geoffrey did not commit himself.

The uncertainty was part of the essence of the legend. In Sir Thomas Malory's *Morte D'Arthur*, which familiarized fifteenth-century readers of English with the Arthurian story, the last words spoken by Arthur are : ' I will into the vale of Avilion, to heal me of my grievous wound. And if thou hear never more of me, pray for my soul'.

THE SOCIAL SCENE IN THE FOURTEENTH CENTURY

By T. Jones Pierce

IT will be recalled that, after his victory in 1282, Edward I retained in his own hands only those parts of Wales out of which he created the first Welsh shires. The counties of Anglesey, Caernarfon, and Merioneth, of Carmarthen, Cardigan, and Flint, were henceforth administered virtually as personal estates of the kings of England — or intermittently, from 1301 onwards, by successive heirs-apparent to the throne of England (1301 being the year when Edward made his son the first English prince of Wales). The rest of Wales continued to be controlled by marcher lords, whose number was increased in 1282 by Edward's action in giving conquered lands in north-east Wales to such leading supporters as the Warrennes, the Lacys, and the Greys. These families now took their place alongside the Mortimers and the Clares, the Bigods and the Bohuns, families which had long been established in the southern and middle marches.

Among these marcher lords there was a sprinkling of Welshmen. Former lords of the principality, they were a mere remnant of an older political dispensation which had for one reason or another survived the débâcle of 1282. But no near relative of the last prince of Wales figured among them. The cadets of the royal house of Gwynedd had languished and died in English fortresses and convents. Alone among the survivors of this family was one of Llywelyn's brothers, Rhodri, a futile and spineless personality who lived out his days as a royal pensioner in Cheshire. But he transmitted some of the fire and spirit of his Gwyndyd ancestry to his grandson, Owain, one of the great military adventurers of the age who, from his exile in France, will emerge later in the century to disturb the English in Wales.

153

Meanwhile further promise of leadership from members of this class appeared slight indeed. A few, such as the La Poles and the D'Avênes (the assumption of frenchified surnames is symptomatic) identified themselves completely with the English marcher lords. The remainder, a mere handful, were small fry with little wealth and following, their diminutive lordships tucked away in remote and poor country. Among them was a certain Gruffydd Fychan, the sole survivor of a group of northern Powysian lords of royal stock. His great-grandson and successor as marcher lord in the upper valley of the Dee was none other than Owain Glyn Dŵr.

In a land inhabited almost exclusively by small peasant proprietors (albeit a land where most peasants considered themselves to be gentlefolk) there were at first few families of native lineage who were in a position to exert much influence on affairs outside their own communities. But there were a few who derived their special position in fourteenth century Wales from official status and favours received at the hands of the native princes ; and who, as we have been told, showed their readiness from the outset to co-operate with the English. With an eye on the spoils of office, the same line was followed by some lesser men without whose assistance, incidentally, foreign civil servants would have been more or less helpless, at a purely local level, in dealing with the mass of a population which was proud and sullen when not openly hostile. As an Englishman of the time once observed, the only way to rule the Welsh was through men of their own race.

These families formed a thin but widely-spread middle layer in the social structure of Wales in the fourteenth century ; they were the vanguard of an indigenous squirearchy who by the time of the Tudors had worked their way up to the summit of Welsh affairs.

The self-interest of this cross-section of Welsh society was glossed, it is true, by loyalties which were a fusion of old and new. Artificially encouraged by successive creations of an English prince of Wales, these loyalties derived a measure of genuine substance later in the century from the fact that for a time it appeared likely that the crown would pass to one who was next in the native line of succession to the principate of the

Llywelyns.   Roger Mortimer, fourth earl of March and heir-
at-law to Richard II (who was also, it will be recalled, a direct
descendant of Gwladus, daughter of Llywelyn the Great), was
hailed by one Welsh poet as a kinsman of the men of Gwynedd,
a worthy successor of the Llywelyns. Roger died in 1398. In
1399 Richard II was deposed and murdered.   In the following
year the great rebellion broke out in Wales.

For several generations past conscripted contingents of
Welshmen had fought on the Scottish borders and the battle-
fields of France.   They were captained by native leaders of pro-
English sentiment, whose martial prowess was praised by their
client bards.   That anti-French and anti-Scottish sentiments
should have replaced the age-old Saxon antipathies in some of
the poems of this period is indicative of the change which had
occurred in certain Welsh social circles.

But there is another side to the picture.   The cumulative
force of record evidence shows that throughout the century
most ordinary Welshmen resented their subjection to alien
rule, and expressed it in their hostility to the official and
' planter ' elements in their midst.   From time to time this
attitude caused tragic and explosive repercussions. At those
moments of crisis the lead, paradoxically, was usually taken by
men who normally leaned towards the Plantagenet connexion
— men whose sympathies had been alienated by the dis-
appointment of their hopes, or by short-sighted opposition
from English officials on the spot.   The most notable examples
of this are Madog ap Llywelyn in 1294, and Owain Glyn Dŵr
in 1400.   On such occasions the protagonists were ranged on a
racial basis, the purely personal issues being merged with a
more general pattern of discontent ; and in the case at least
of the crises to which special reference has been made, merged
with older dynastic loyalties.   As at the beginning, so at the end
of the century, there were minds at work which were familiar
in every detail with that conception of Welsh statehood which
had animated the policies of Llywelyn the Great, and which
had been brought to fruition for a fleeting decade by Llywelyn
ap Gruffydd.

We cannot ignore the episode already foreshadowed when,
in the thirteen-seventies, Owain ap Rhodri became a pawn in

the Anglo-French struggle. The proclamation which he made as he was about to set out with a French fleet on a threatened invasion of Wales shows a sure grasp of his historic claims to the realm of Wales by right and descent from his ancestors, kings of that country. Far less can we ignore the evidence of protracted and widespread official alarm in Wales during those years, and of secret preparations for rebellion if Owain had succeeded in landing on these shores ; and of the posthumous appeal of his name for those Welshmen who had rested their hopes on his advent.

This antithesis of feeling towards alien authority colours in some measure most aspects of life in Wales during the fourteenth century, and considerably aggravated the social and economic tensions caused by the reshaping of Welsh medieval society in this period.

The English authorities did not, of course, at once sweep away all they found in the new shires and lordships of north and west Wales. They preferred to leave the slow processes of time to leaven society with the novel things which were introduced with the conquest. One drastic step was the substitution of money rents tied to tribal lands for the traditional services and food tributes of the people. This had already happened among the upland tribesmen in the old lordships of the south. Now, over the rest of Wales, old customs, which for generations had been an intimate part of life in the Welsh countryside, and which had been found a convenient way of exacting dues when native rulers were resident in those parts, disappeared for ever. Absentee princes and marcher lords were only interested in the cash value of those ancient customs. Indeed, officials from England (with strange-sounding names such as sheriff, steward, receiver, and the like), who, throughout the fourteenth century, administered these territories at the higher levels, were above all else expected, like their counterparts in the old-established lordships of the south, to make these financial arrangements work. Shire and lordship were in the first place estates to be exploited for the material benefit of absentee princes and marcher lords. This became increasingly true as the fourteenth century drew to a close.

So revolutionary a change in a society which, as a Welshman

of that period once said, had very little use for money, could not have worked without something being done to increase the circulation of money through increased trade and exchange. With a view to encouraging the Welsh to trade and use money more extensively than in the past, the system of urban 'plantations,' which had long existed in the southern march lands, was introduced into north and mid-Wales. In the shadows of the new castles, which the conquerors built for their protection and as centres of higher administration, at places like Caernarfon, Conway, Flint, Builth, and Aberystwyth, walled towns appeared. And these were ' planted ' by colonists from England who were given, among other privileges, exclusive trading rights among the rural Welsh of their area.

Constrained by these innovations into new attitudes of mind, the average Welshman could not but resent the proximity of these isolated foreign outposts sheltering officials and traders who, to his mind, were to blame for harsh intrusions on cherished habits.

For a generation or so adjustment to the abrupt change-over in fiscal methods pressed hardly on Welsh society. Before the wheels of commerce began to turn fast enough many a small hill tribesman had lost to authority his entire working stock of cattle in lieu of unpaid rents. In coastal areas where tribesmen were more familiar with cash transactions, the transition was less severe except among the serfs. So high were the rents imposed on this unfortunate minority, because the customs which they had once rendered had been particularly burdensome, that there began those periodic flights which by the close of the century had brought this class to the point of extinction.

Officials often tried to extract more than was strictly due, and the resulting tension was hardly lessened when officials discovered that there were Welshmen who were expert at the art of tax evasion. There was also irritation in the shires at the introduction, lock, stock and barrel, of inquisitorial methods of government which were tending to become outmoded in England. Intended ostensibly to secure information and discourage lawlessness, this machinery in the long run became unduly oppressive in that it was exploited as a source of increased emoluments by way of fines — often very heavy fines imposed on whole communities of Welshmen.

All tenants of tribal lands, moreover, were compelled to make frequent attendance, involving much wearisome travel, at shire and seigneurial courts which in the Middle Ages, it should be realised, were as much administrative as judicial institutions. This was so overwhelming a source of grievance that attendance at the more important courts was limited in time to tribesmen whose stake in the soil was relatively large. This was a step which eventually brought a measure of gain. The wealthier tribesmen who continued to attend supplied in every shire and lordship a nucleus of continuous collective experience of public affairs — experience which, as medieval methods of government passed into decay, was transmitted to the rising native gentry who were called upon in the sixteenth century to shoulder, as justices of the peace, the entire burden of local government in Wales.

Furthermore, to touch on a vast and complex subject, official opposition to the continued use in the courts of the law of Hywel Dda did not meet with the same success in the lordships where Welsh law lingered on into the fifteenth century, as in the shires. By the middle of the century English law had won the day on royal territory over all fields of legal administration except in disputes over tribal land, where Welshmen as a whole preferred to make use of native arbitrators versed in the complexities of tribal custom, as indeed Edward I had conceded in the ordinances of 1284.

Then at the very moment when Welshmen were beginning to get used to the new order (the more adventurous were even breaking away from their old roots and seeking a new existence in the boroughs), and when English residents were starting to find their adopted land less strange and astonishing (such were the words used by an early settler) than they had done at first, the Great Pestilence ravaged the country in 1349 and 1350. This calamity, followed as it was in later years by further outbreaks of plague, upset the balance of the old rural economy throughout the marchlands and the shires, quickened the tempo of social change, revived old and created new discontents.

A sharp fall in population and a long period of low prices threatened the incomes of royal government and marcher aristocracy alike. That their henchmen in Wales were able to the very end of the century to keep customary revenues more or less at the old figure reflects, as the records themselves reveal, a new phase of administrative pressure. The suffering which this entailed was by no means an evenly distributed burden. The unfree who had to pay rents for their brethren who had disappeared through death or flight, the small and middling tribesman, embarrassed by depressed markets for his surplus produce and by a diminishing stake in tribal lands brought about by the Welsh practice of divided inheritance, even the trader with little capital with which to surmount a period of economic crisis, these people were all caught between the demands of officials and the cupidity of richer burgesses and tribesmen. In the general social dislocation of the times, this upper middle element in society saw the opportunity, as it turned out, to start building the estates on which rested the power of their successors in a later age. Everywhere, and particularly in the tribal borderlands between Flint and north Pembroke, we see them buying small holdings and reshaping the hamlets, in which hitherto groups of clansmen held shares, into modern consolidated farms.

In a setting peculiar to Wales, social solvents were at work which were simultaneously changing the pattern of society elsewhere in the west, and not least of all in the anglicised manors of the Welsh march lands.

In conclusion it may be added that, difficult though it may be to do more than guess how the immediate occasions of the Glyn Dŵr rising fit into the web of general discontent, regarded from the standpoint of those who refused to identify themselves with English rule, the rebellion was the final protest of a proud and conservative peasantry against the interaction of alien institutions and money economy with their former tribal way of living.

RELIGION IN MEDIEVAL WALES

By Glanmor Williams

LATE in the fifteenth century the Welsh poet, Guto'r Glyn, lay
tossing restlessly on his bed. His imagination played uneasily
over meditations on death and the hereafter. The sound of
the trumpet at the Last Judgment resounded in his head and
dragged him from his slumber.

> " Mae corn y frawd i'm cern fry,
> A'm geilw yma o'm gwely."

For Guto, the eternal world was tremendously real, more real
almost than the world around him. He had a terrifyingly clear
mental picture of the Last Judgment and of the torments of
Hell and Purgatory, and a more hazy notion of the bliss of
Heaven he hoped to attain. Sermons, pictures, sculptures,
stained glass, books, and traditions, all impressed upon
medieval man the overwhelming responsibility of the destiny
of his soul. They also taught him that that responsibility could
be discharged only through the Church. He believed without
demur that only by accepting the sacraments and the teaching
of the Church and its ministers could he attain salvation. This
did not prevent him from being at times flippant, sacrilegious
or critical. He might be irritated by the jurisdiction of the
courts of the Church and resentful at the burden of its financial
exactions. He might break its commandments and scamp or
evade the duties he owed it. But he would not as a rule care to
flout its ultimate sanction : that it alone held the keys of
eternal life and the safeguards against everlasting damnation.

Its sacraments met him at all the great turning-points of his
life. His physical birth was paralleled by the sacrament of
baptism. When he came to manhood his bishop administered
the corresponding religious rite of confirmation. He came to

11. Talley Abbey

church to have his union with a wife solemnized by the sacrament of marriage. As he approached the threshold of death he received forgiveness of mortal sins when extreme unction was administered to him. Just as his body had to have food so his soul needed the sustenance of mass ; and just as his bodily ailments needed healing so the disorders of his soul must be cleansed by the sacrament of penance.

For all the passing seasons of the year the Church had its Christian calendar. At all the great festivals there were appropriate services and ceremonies. At Christmas, churches and houses were brightened by silent representations of the scene at Bethlehem. Ashes were received on Ash Wednesday as a token of the defilement of sin. On Palm Sunday the congregation bore palms and sang " Hosanna" to welcome a procession of priests. On Good Friday and Easter Sunday they re-enacted the burial and resurrection of Jesus. There was no point in human life to which the influence of the Church did not penetrate. Public health, charity, education, scholarship, and the arts ; all fell beneath its sway. It very largely created the medieval civilization, of which churches great and small are the most characteristic memorials.

So great was the spiritual and intellectual authority of the Church and so extensive its possessions that, in the eleventh century, when the Normans came to Wales, they were bound to try to exercise control over it. In Wales they found a Church which was still markedly Celtic in character. Its discipline and institutions differed widely from those with which the Normans were familiar. This was a state of affairs which the intruders would tolerate no longer than they had to. Pious, according to their lights, as well as practical, they were able to reinforce their political need to control the Church with an agreeable sense of a religious mission to introduce reform. The individual lords who carried out the conquest piecemeal were not the only ones to realize the need for controlling the Church. The king of England and his archbishop of Canterbury were no less aware of its importance.

The first step, from which all else might follow, was to gain control over the election of bishops. In 1107, Urban the first Norman bishop of Llandaff, was induced to make the first profession of obedience to the see of Canterbury. This set the pattern for the future. By the middle of the twelfth century bishops of all four Welsh dioceses had been induced to make this profession. The first and decisive stage of bringing the Welsh Church under the control of king and archbishop had been accomplished. It was a change big with consequences for Church and people, comparable in scope and magnitude with those later to be brought about by the Protestant Reformation and the Methodist Revival.

This new relationship between the Welsh bishops and Canterbury was not readily accepted in Wales. The princes of Gwynedd, following the line set by Owain Gwynedd in the twelfth century, regarded the diocese of Bangor as their own special preserve and were unwilling to allow the influence of Canterbury to be extended over the see. In south Wales Gerald the Welshman, himself three parts a Norman, was to become the most vigorous champion of the right of the Welsh Church to independence of Canterbury. For a quarter of a century from 1176 onwards he fought a campaign to have St. David's recognized as the seat of an archbishopric independent of Canterbury. Quarrelsome, witty, voluble, opinionated, eloquent, conceited and indefatigable, Gerald pleaded his case in season and out of season, in St. David's and at the papal curia, among clergy and laity. Flattering, castigating, persuading and exhorting, he employed all the resources of one of the liveliest tongues and swiftest pens known to the Middle Ages. And all, alas, in vain !

Another major step taken by the Normans to destroy the Celtic organization of the Church was to break up the *clas* wherever possible. The *clas* consisted of a body of canons, usually hereditary, attached to a mother church. Wherever the Normans were strongly established, *clasau* were suppressed and their endowments transferred to monasteries in England or on the Continent. In this way the venerable *clas* founded by Illtud at Llantwit Major perished and its possessions passed to the abbey of Tewkesbury.

Closely connected with this step of breaking up the *clasau* was the introduction of Latin type monasteries into Wales. The first to be founded were those of the Benedictine order. Found only along the Normanized fringes and built in the shadow of Norman castles, they were almost as much an instrument of conquest as the castle or borough. Not one Benedictine house flourished in those parts of Wales held for any length of time by the Welsh princes. To the end of their existence the Black Monks in Wales were recruited from a non-Welsh population.

But we should be getting an entirely false perspective of the medieval Church if we thought of it only as an instrument of political subjection. The impact of the Norman Conquest also had immense consequences for good. The isolation of the pre-Norman church in Wales carried with it the peril of stagnation as the price of autonomy. By breaking down this isolation the Normans threw the Church open to fresh and invigorating streams of reform flowing strongly from the Continent. One of the most decisive consequences was to bring the Welsh Church into more intimate relationship with the fountainhead of medieval religion, the reformed papacy. To Rome the most active and zealous Welsh clerics looked for inspiration and guidance. From Rome came much of the driving force behind the transforming of the organization and government of the Church in Wales.

This transformation is indeed the most enduring achievement of the medieval Church. One of the first tasks was to change the mother-daughter relationship of Celtic bishoprics into territorially-defined dioceses. That is, instead of a bishop having authority over a number of widely-scattered churches which regarded his church as their mother-church, he now ruled over a fixed geographical area. Within these territorial dioceses, other new ecclesiastical boundaries were being mapped out. Archdeaconries and rural deaneries came into being for the first time. The rural deanery was usually based on the civil unit of the commote or the cantref, and the archdeaconry on a province. Parishes, too, were being carved out on a territorial basis for the first time — a slow and difficult job which was not completed in north Wales until well on into the fourteenth century.

One of the main purposes of the new territorial organization of the Church was to pave the way for the introduction of stricter canons of discipline. In this process the archdeacons

and rural deans were to be the key men. They were usually of
Welsh origin and in close touch with priests and people. But
theirs was no easy task. Progress was slow, and compromises
and failures were inevitable. There was one notoriously difficult problem on which the disciplinary machine always tended
to break its teeth. That was the celibacy of the clergy. The
Church found it impossible to enforce this generally, and right
down to the eve of the Reformation most Welsh parish priests
took wives.

The ideal of celibacy found more willing adherents among
the religious orders. I have spoken of the failure of the Benedictines to make any impression on the Welsh. But the
Cistercians or White Monks were conspicuously successful.
This was chiefly because they were not associated in Welsh
minds with alien conquest. Far from being timid henchmen
of the Normans who clung to the skirts of castle and borough,
the Cistercians sought out the solitude of mountain and moorland. Their austere discipline seemed to reincarnate the ideals
of the Celtic saints. Their emphasis on pastoral farming fitted
well into the stock-rearing economy of Wales, though not as
smoothly and unresentedly as is sometimes suggested. The
Cistercians won a unique place in the affections of princes and
people. Their houses became havens of ordered worship,
cradles of learning, patrons of literature, and pioneers in the
arts of flock-management and wool production. Names like
Strata Florida, Conway, Valle Crucis, Margam and Tintern
are among the most hallowed in the history of religion in
medieval Wales.

By the thirteenth century the initiative among religious
orders was tending to pass to the new orders of friars. The
friars moved freely among the people, the Franciscans in their
grey habit, and the Dominicans in black. Both orders were
very well received in Wales. From their midst were drawn
some of the foremost scholars and bishops of medieval Wales.
Such a one was Anian, bishop of St. Asaph from 1268 to
1293. This fiery Dominican came from a line of princes and
warriors. Thin-skinned, hot-blooded, and obstinate, a tremendous stickler for the rights of his see, he was willing to press
his claims against Welsh abbots or English bishops, king

Edward I or prince Llywelyn the Last. And he fought with all
the reckless and dedicated ardour of a churchman convinced
his cause was Heaven's. Another notable friar was John
Wallensis or John the Welshman. He was one of the earliest
regent-masters of the Franciscan order at Oxford and was later
regent-master at Paris University, where he was known a
Arbor Vitae (" tree of life"). He was a prolific author and his
sermon collections were among the most popular compendia
of their kind in the Middle Ages.

Friars formed only a small proportion of the Welsh students
at the universities. Though no university had emerged in
Wales itself enterprising young Welshmen were finding their
way to Paris and other centres of European learning from the
twelfth century onwards. They made their way in still larger
numbers to Oxford once that great university had been founded.
All these students were clerics or would-be clerics. Laymen
did not, as a rule, bother with university education during the
Middle Ages.

But the learning of these clerics was not confined to a small
élite reading Latin. One of the most remarkable achievements
of the medieval Church was to produce a large body of literature in the vernacular which the less well educated clergy and
laity might understand. Parts of the Bible were translated into
Welsh ; so were the Creed, the more popular hymns and
prayers, the lives of the saints, and works of devotion and
mysticism. These prose translations were well known to the
poets of Wales and had a powerful impact on their verse. The
poets frequently wrote on religious subjects. Their favourite
themes are few and simple, and recur again and again. Chief
among them were praise of the Trinity, and especially the
sufferings of Christ, terror of the Last Judgment and Hell —
this was perhaps the most persistent and awe-inspiring motif ;
the brevity and brittleness of human life, confession of sins, and
devotion to the Virgin and the saints.

All this gives enough evidence of the vigour of the medieval
Church at its best. But by the middle of the fourteenth century
it becomes apparent that the most creative and fruitful period
is passing and decline is setting in. The most important reasons
for this affect Christendom as a whole and I can mention them

only very briefly. Among them were the decline of the papacy, the break-up of the thirteenth-century synthesis of philosophy and religion, the cooling ardour of the religious orders, and the re-assertion of the claims of the secular state. But there are also other reasons which more particularly affect England and Wales.

First among these I should place the growing subordination of the interests of the Church to those of State. In the fourteenth century the king drew nearly all his leading civil servants from among the clergy. He rewarded them by giving them bishoprics and other high preferment in the Church. This tended to make them more and more administrators and politicians, absent from their sees and incapable of giving them pastoral direction. The position was all the worse in Wales because Welsh clerics were as a rule excluded from the highest preferment there. This built up a strong sense of resentment and frustration which was to find violent expression in the Glyn Dŵr rebellion.

Another important factor was the seemingly interminable Hundred Years' War with France. This led the king to exploit the Church still more intensively in the interests of the State. It also had a very bad effect on the leading religious order in Wales, the Cistercians, who were now cut off from their mother house in France and whose discipline and standards suffered badly.

To complicate matters still further came the Black Death and other plagues whose repeated visitations hit the Church hard. The numbers of the clergy were sharply reduced and replacements that were hastily drafted in were of poorer quality.

All these difficulties had the effect of producing a very severe economic crisis by the end of the fourteenth century. The Church and its clergy, no less than the laity, were now undergoing tremendous pressure from changing social and economic circumstances. They were in bitter and rebellious mood. It needed only a spark to touch off an explosion.

When Owain Glyn Dŵr raised the standard of rebellion the Welsh clergy flocked to support him. This rebellion bristles with thorny problems. I can touch upon only one : Owain's plan for an independent archbishopric and independent universities for Wales. This was not, as is often thought, a bold and advanced plan for religious and educational reform. It was an integral part of Owain's political programme. If he was going to run an independent state he had to have trained administrators. They could come only from the clergy and would have to be paid. The object of the Welsh universities was to provide Owain with an independent source of supply of civil servants, and the independent archbishopric would furnish the means of paying them. As we know, the rebellion failed. In the course of it the Church had suffered untold losses. Its buildings and possessions were devastated ; discipline was shattered ; learning was at its lowest ebb. The monastery of Margam was in 1412 described as " utterly destroyed so that abbot and convent are obliged to go about like vagabonds." Its destitution was typical of the Welsh Church as a whole at this time.

Gradually, during the fifteenth century, some measure of recovery was achieved. Materially, its losses had been made good by 1500. Spiritually, recovery was much less complete. The greatest signs of vigour are to be seen in the less admirable aspects of medieval religion : uncritical veneration of the saints, pilgrimages, relics, and so on. The more enlightened trends of contemporary mysticism or of Catholic humanism find little echo in medieval Wales. For the majority religion consisted of a mass of traditional assumptions and practices, unquestioningly accepted but dimly apprehended. Habit rather than conviction was the most powerful element in the faith of the *gwerin* on the eve of the Reformation changes. This left them as ill-prepared to defend the old as to welcome the new in face of the storm that was soon to break on them.

DAFYDD AP GWILYM

By Thomas Parry

PROFESSOR Gwyn Jones has described the Mabinogion as " our real contribution to medieval prose romance." I shall say something about our real contribution to medieval poetry.

Of Dafydd ap Gwilym's life very little is known, and very little need be known. He lived in the middle of the fourteenth century and was a member of a well established and influential west Wales family whose home was originally in Pembrokeshire, though the poet was born in north Cardiganshire. Being a nobleman he was probably never engaged in any strenuous occupation, except that the production of the type of poetry which he wrote was in itself a pretty strenuous job. He was free to travel, and was obviously familiar with all parts of Wales. He sang of Newborough in Anglesey, Bangor, Caernarfon, and knew all the rivers and the ferries between the modern Portmadoc and St. David's. He had been to Maelor in Denbighshire, Ceri and Llanllugan in Montgomeryshire, and at the end of a life of wandering, jesting and a wholehearted devotion to the artistry of words he found a grave at Strata Florida abbey, under a yew tree which is the subject of a charming poem by his friend Gruffudd Gryg.

To appreciate the poetry of Dafydd ap Gwilym one first step is indispensable : we must rid ourselves completely of that conception of the function of poetry which we may have inherited from the Romantic movement. To Dafydd ap Gwilym (as to his contemporary, Geoffrey Chaucer) poetry is not intended to justify the ways of God to man, nor to reconcile the ways of man to God. It is not the outpourings of the master spirit intent upon a sublime self-expression or upon the sublimation of a degraded self. The poet is not the builder of the new Jerusalem. Poetry is concerned with no problem, no propaganda, be that political, religious or humanitarian. The poet is no visionary or prophet : Carlyle's hero as poet would be fantastic and utterly incomprehensible in the fourteenth century. To Dafydd ap Gwilym poetry is entertainment. It is not the entertainment of the theatre of Ibsen, Galsworthy and Bernard Shaw, but more akin to a play by Christopher Fry, with all its improbable situations, its abundance of wit and verbal gymnastics — *Venus Observed,* for example. There you have something which it is quite legitimate to compare with the poetry of Dafydd ap Gwilym, in both its aim and its expression.

To understand what Dafydd ap Gwilym was doing when he wrote poetry we must grasp the salient fact that he was essentially a performer, and that he addressed an audience. There are several passages in his poems which prove that they were read or recited or sung in the great hall or in the solarium, where the nobleman and his retainers, or perhaps just he and his family, were entertained. Like all entertainers Dafydd depended for his success on two main elements : first, the content or substance of his act — what he actually says in his poem; and secondly, his skill or dexterity in presentation. And I am going to try to show how this Welsh poet utilized all the resources of his extremely fertile imagination and also his amazing mastery of word and idiom to delight his fellow men and women.

Broadly speaking, Dafydd's two main themes were love and nature. A large number of Dafydd's poems was written to two women, whom he constantly mentions by name. Let me make it quite clear at the outset that it is my firm opinion that they were real women of flesh and blood, known personally to Dafydd and to all his acquaintances. To imagine that they were fictitious names, merely the creations of the poet's imagination, is to invest fourteenth-century customs with nineteenth-century prudery. If these women were not real, then Dafydd's poetry would lose all its social significance and the element of comedy which is its very essence.

Let us first of all consider Dyddgu. She is the daughter of Ieuan ap Gruffudd ap Llywelyn, a woman of high birth, gentle and considerate, skilled in various occupations, endowed with all the virtues of womanhood, well spoken and well regarded. Dafydd courts her ardently and often, but to no avail. He never succeeds in winning her affection, and yet her very aloofness enhances her charm. The eight poems which he addressed to her are in a tradition well established in Wales and ultimately traceable to the works of the troubadour poets of Provence in the twelfth century. It is the essence of this literary tradition that a poet should profess love for a noble woman, and express it in noble poetry. Such was the love professed by Cynddelw in the twelfth century for Eve, and by Llywarch ap Llywelyn for Nest, daughter of Hywel. It was the assumption of the age — a not unreasonable one — that the finest sentiment a man may feel for a woman is the sentiment of love, the highest honour he can pay her is to make her the object of his affection. We need not believe that the poet feels all that he professes ; probably the woman addressed did not believe it either. But this is of no consequence. Mere questions of veracity pale into contemptible insignificance alongside the honour which a noble lady receives by being addressed in terms of love by a poet who is of rank equivalent to her own. It is this honour that Dafydd pays to Dyddgu. In one poem he confesses to an overweening ambition in ever having paid suit to her, but hopes that one day, when all her suitors have deserted her, he may be successful. In another poem he greets her father, thanking him for his very generous welcome the other night, for gifts of gold, sparkling wine, mead, braggett and very good cheer generally. There is only one fault with the nobleman's household, and that is that his daughter, Dyddgu, will not respond to the poet's professions of love. In all the poems to Dyddgu she is spoken of with the highest respect, and furthermore they are all written in the poet's best style, with all the rhetorical embellishments and metrical intricacies of which he was capable. To us it may all seem like disingenuous flattery, but it was nothing of the sort to the men and women of the fourteenth century. It was a courteous social custom, a form of polite entertainment. And let me say once more that it would have been utterly meaningless had not Dyddgu been a living person.

We will now turn to Morfudd, who is the very antithesis of all that Dyddgu is. She is excitable, coquettish, fickle and utterly unreliable, but ravishingly beautiful and supremely

attractive. Dafydd sums her up in two very significant words —
a glowing ember, that is, she is brilliant and ardent. Unlike
Dyddgu, she easily responds to the poet's advances ; he wins
her, only to lose her again when a more impressive admirer
catches her eye. She is eventually married to the Little Hunch-
back (*Y Bwa Bach*), and Dafydd swears never to have anything
more to do with her, but this promise is broken many a time
and the husband is obliged to guard his prize very jealously
indeed. Here again we have a real person, because the husband,
Y Bwa Bach, is mentioned by this very nickname in a legal
document of 1344.

Dafydd wrote about thirty poems to Morfudd, and she is the
source of boundless merriment and pretended anguish. He
exults because she has given him a garland of birch leaves as a
token of her love for him. She sends him a present of nuts as
another token of her affection, much to the poet's delight. She
placed her two arms around his neck, and he devotes a whole
poem to say how blissful it is to be thus shackled and to be
drunk with love.

But these bouts of being obliging and manageable were
unfortunately very rare. Much more often Morfudd is re-
fractory and supercilious. On a miserable night of sleet and
snow she refused to unlock her door and left the poet, poor
man, to stand beneath her window with the drip from the eaves
falling on the nape of his neck and chilling his very marrow.
He, of course, sensible man that he is, would never have been
out at all on such a night were it not for her. She flits from one
lover to another, like a ball being tossed from hand to hand.
Dafydd once loved her dearly and spent his gift of song for her
sake, gave her jewels and personal ornaments, entertained her
lavishly with wine in the tavern and with mead at the inn, but
she gave not a thing in return. Indeed she has gone and got
married, and all Dafydd's friends poke fun at him for being
such a fool. Now he is sighing till his breast is almost bursting ;
each sigh is sufficient to blow out a candle, and people think by
the noise he makes that he is a piper. He heaves like a black-
smith's bellows and the air that he exhales is enough to winnow
corn.

The Jealous Husband, who is constantly deceived and

thwarted, enters into many of Dafydd's poems, other than the ones to Morfudd. The poet rejoices that he is able to entice the young wife out into the woods and the fields where her husband will not be able to find them. Another lovely girl newly married to a loathsome old man is already showing signs of deterioration. Conspicuous blemishes appear in her complexion, and she is at a loss to know what to do about it. Dafydd first of all explains the reason for this sad state of affairs, which is, that the husband's filthy breath discolours and tarnishes the girl's complexion. For, says he, a varnished wooden image in church is damaged if the smoke from a candle gets at it ; the finest English ermine is spoilt by peat smoke ; all the sun's brilliance is hidden by fog ; a flourishing young oak tree withers away if exposed to salt breezes from the sea. Dafydd then suggests a remedy, much cheaper and more efficacious than any modern cleansing cream or powder base — let the girl elope with him.

Dafydd's main source of diversion was to picture himself in a false position or an embarrassing and undignified situation, thus making himself the butt of the company's laughter. He was once spending a night at a common lodging house, where he spotted a most adorable girl. He treated her to good roast and choice wines and suggested they might meet again after all the others had gone to sleep. On his way to the girl, however, he fell, striking his leg against a stool and his head against a trestle table, which was upset, and a huge brass pan fell to the floor with a terrific din. This woke up three Englishmen — Hickin, Jenkin and Jack — who were sleeping in a stinking bed, and who immediately raised the alarm, thinking that a burglar had entered the house. Dafydd lay low in the darkness, offering a prayer, and through the grace of the Lord Jesus and the intercession of the saints, he managed to escape, and begged God for His forgiveness.

The other aspect of Dafydd ap Gwilym's poetic genius is his powers of expression and technical ability. It may reasonably be asked to what extent did the technical skill displayed in Dafydd's poems contribute to their value as entertainment in the halls of the nobility where they were first sung or recited. Would a contemporary audience be able to appreciate the metaphors, the similes, the covert references and all the nuances of poetic diction which a modern reader can study and respond to at leisure ? It is safe to say, I think, that it was the content of the poem that appealed most forcibly — the amatory adventure related, the predicaments and embarrassing situations in which the poet found himself, his profession of love for a tantalizing beauty or his righteous denunciation of a jealous husband. These things Dafydd's public would immediately recognize and appreciate.

But we must not forget the high proficiency of the performer, which I have already mentioned. The performer's very skill and executant ability is always a source of wonder and a potent element in every entertainment, and we can well imagine that Dafydd's audience enjoyed a poem of between thirty and forty lines all beginning with the same consonant, or another of similar length on one rhyme throughout. The sheer cleverness of a performance of this kind excites admiration. Another device which no doubt kept Dafydd's audience interested was his practice of drawing comparisons between the subject of his poem and various other objects, many of them often far-fetched and grotesque. For example, the mountain mist which overtook him on his journey to meet the girl he loved is like a roll of parchment, a rusty sieve, a net for catching birds, a sheet of cloth extending from one end of the sky to the other, a monk's cowl, a thick grey fleece, the rain's coat of mail, a cloak of fur, the lofty battlements of the fairies, the smoke of torches reaching into the stars, the whole world struck with blindness, an immense spider's web, steam from the forest like that from the backs of horses, the bath of the witches of the underworld.

In contrast to this piling up of imagery, Dafydd sometimes uses just one or two similes which, through their aptness and the prominence given them, acquire a very high significance. Morfudd is now old ; she, who had once captivated men, she whose beauty and allurement had kept the poet and many another awake at night thinking of her ; the Creator himself has made her old and ugly. The poem ends with two similes : one is " the rod of a mangonel." Some of you may know something of medieval artillery and that the mangonel was a contraption for hurling stones at the enemy's fortifications. It consisted of a supple tree trunk firmly fixed in a timber frame. With a winch and a rope the tree trunk could be bent backwards and then suddenly released, and in straightening itself it provided an impetus to the stone missile which was attached to it.   Morfudd crooked with age was like this bent tree trunk, and the comparison implies not only the crookedness of her body but also a certain pent-up viciousness.   This simile was, in Dafydd's time, very modern, as if somebody to-day were to mention a Sten gun or a jet plane.   The sons of the nobility who had followed the Black Prince to the French wars would have seen many a mangonel.

Another characteristic of Dafydd ap Gwilym's poems which I am sure would greatly affect his audience is the dialogue which he so often introduces into them.   This brings in a live dramatic element.   The poet is walking about in the forest on a bright April morning expecting the arrival of the girl he loves. Nearby is a magpie, busily building its nest, who says to Dafydd, " What is all this fuss about ? A man of your age had better be sitting by the fire at home than getting his feet wet in the morning dew." Dafydd replies, " Leave me alone. It is my great love for a fair maid that brings me here." " An old fogey like you," says the magpie, " stands no chance. All this talk about a pretty girl is only self-deception." Dafydd replies, " The devil it is. If you pretend to so much wisdom, give me some advice for this grave affliction I am in." " I will give you excellent advice. You don't deserve a fair maid. There is only one advice that is suitable : become a monk, retire to a monastery and give up loving women." The poem concludes with Dafydd swearing that if ever he finds a magpie's nest he will tear it to pieces and smash up all the eggs.

These conversation pieces remind one of the Mabinogi and the other tales of medieval Wales, in which dialogue plays a very prominent part.

Dafydd's poems are not only clever entertainment for the men of his own age ; by virtue of his exuberant inventiveness, his fertility of imagery and his sense of the unity of a poem he is the poet of every age.   He was also a supreme master of versification.   The rules of Welsh prosody which governed Dafydd's versification were probably the most intricate and exacting that any poet ever had to contend with. The repetition of consonants demanded by *cynghanedd*, the rhyme schemes, together with other metrical complications which Dafydd chose to impose upon himself, would have been enough to stifle the very breath out of a man of lesser ability.   But he transcends all difficulties ; indeed he turns them to advantage ; and into the seemingly dry bones of a perplexing metrical system he breathes the spirit of fine poetry.

OWAIN GLYN DŴR

By Gwyn A. Williams

ON the 16th of September, 1400, a group of rebels gathered outside Ruthin and proclaimed their leader, Owain Glyn Dŵr, prince of Wales, in armed defiance of Henry of Lancaster, who had deposed Richard II and assumed the crown as Henry IV. By this act, they unleashed a savage conflict, which raged for ten years and more, devastated Wales, and created an independent Welsh principality, the first to enjoy spontaneous popular support from the whole country, whose final collapse left ruins to affront the eyes, bitter memories to trouble the minds, of the Welsh.

With the Glyn Dŵr rising, this small people — scarcely more than 200,000 strong — made its own contribution to the convulsions which wracked western Christendom in the period — the French Jacquerie, the English Peasants' Revolt, the Hussite wars. For the basic cause was the same — the emergence of new classes, modern forms of social organisation from the dissolving fabric of the medieval order. In the march of Wales, as in baronial England, under the impact of plague and slump, manorial structure was disintegrating. A class of richer peasants was clawing its way up, while less fortunate colleagues went to the wall, as the modern pattern of squire-tenant-labourer relationships began to take shape, in embryo. In the crown lands, the Principality, under the pressure of new monetary influences radiating from the plantation boroughs, and with the continuous expansion necessary to its smooth working no longer possible in many areas, the kindred as a closely-knit land-holding unit was losing its integrity, its structure riddled, honeycombed with intruders, distorted by the rise of a new class — the gentry in course of formation.

And, cutting across this process of social change, was the continuous pressure of the state and private landlords. In the

Principality, the unfree, less than a tenth of the population, supplied some two-thirds of the royal revenue, and the attempt to force a money economy on this area where production geared to a market was hardly known, made their lives well-nigh intolerable. Similarly in the march, the stricken lords turned to the profits of their courts to make up for their losses in the fields. They proved remarkably successful. The population of England may have fallen by as much as thirty per cent in the late fourteenth century ; baronial income fell, if at all, by less than ten per cent. This peculiar conjuncture of social mobility and judicial counter-attack, aggravated by no fewer than ten serious outbreaks of bubonic plague, proved explosive. In England, it produced the Peasants' Revolt of 1381. In Wales, the crisis of the English manors was reproduced, with the added ingredient of racial hostility. In both march and Principality, it was the anger of the unfree which gave the Glyn Dŵr rising its destructive ferocity.

This is the reality underlying the Glyn Dŵr movement. Throughout Wales, a new society was emerging from the cracking shell of the old — and a bewildered peasantry struck out blindly at what it considered to be the agents of the change. It found scapegoats, in the planted English borough, in the alien officer, in the whole political establishment, and in those Welshmen who collaborated with it. In reaction, it found refuge in a deepened sense of nationality, a sense of national identity, which finds its clearest expression in the verses of the bards. For the bardic order, last repository of the old traditions, focussed now on the households of the gentry, preached to that gentry, year in year out, the virtues of the old Welsh aristocratic ideal. More than any other agency, it gave shape to the form-less angers released by social change, channelled thought to a political outlook, centring on a restoration of Welsh honour and a prince of Welsh blood. And, from time to time, from Madoc's rising through to the days of Owen of Wales, government in Wales was paralysed by spasmodic outbreaks of this feeling.

To translate discontent into sustained purpose, however, was a political action. Such action could originate only among the Welsh gentry. This was a class divided in its loyalties. Typical of many was that gentleman who changed his coat of arms at the conquest — replacing his former three bloody Saxons' heads with the more tactful three closed helmets. In the rising, brother fought brother at Caernarfon ; Glyn Dŵr's own cousin was his enemy. The revolt bore all the stigmata of civil war.

In north Wales at this time, decision rested with an influential Anglesey clan, whom we can identify with the name one of its branches later made famous — the Tudors. One of the traditional stocks, the Tudors had collaborated with the new regime, and, with their extensive marriage connexions, the five sons of Tudur ap Gronw in the late fourteenth century commanded a powerful bloc or connexion among the official Welsh aristocracy. But they had always been prickly, and the key to the situation in 1400 lies in their reaction to political fluctuations in England. For Richard II had been as popular in Wales as in Cheshire, and Gwilym and Rhys Tudor, in particular, seem to have enjoyed some kind of personal relationship with the unfortunate king. His overthrow in 1399, therefore, was a particularly brutal affront to a sensitive sector of Welsh opinion. If Henry IV's usurpation was going to cause trouble in Wales, it was from the Tudor connexion it would come.

And from this connexion it did come, for Owain Glyn Dŵr was a member of it. The Tudor brothers were his cousins. But Owain was rather a special member. Through his father, he was descended directly from the princes of northern Powys; through his mother, from those of south Wales. Wales at this time was strewn with the rubble of its ancient dynasties, but if the Welsh were looking for a true-blooded prince of traditional stock they could find no better candidate.

But he was also a lord of the march, holding Glyn Dyfrdwy and Cynllaith Owain, near the Dee, directly of the king by Welsh barony. His wife was one of the Flintshire Hanmers, English marcher stock ; one of his daughters married John Scudamore of that famous Herefordshire family. Owain was, in short, a member of that mixed marcher society which has so dominated our history. And with a comfortable income of around £200 a year, he was a complete gentleman of the period. He served his term as law student at the Inns of Court — a finishing school for the upper classes — and in 1386, appeared as witness before a celebrated court of chivalry, in company with the poet Geoffrey Chaucer and indistinguishable from the throng of gilded baronial youth. He had served in the Scots campaign of 1385, wearing his scarlet flamingo feather and driving the Scots before him like goats, according to the bard. He served in other campaigns too, probably in the retinue of his powerful neighbour, the earl of Arundel, possibly even under Henry of Lancaster himself. For there is no positive evidence to link Glyn Dŵr with Richard II. Here he differs from his Tudor cousins. This is the first mystery.

About his neighbour, however, there is no mystery. Reginald de Grey, lord of Ruthin, was an intimate of the new king. And during 1399–1400, relations between Grey and Glyn Dŵr became envenomed. The quarrel was probably over land ; Grey had the ear of the king ; Welshmen, as supporters of Richard, were suspect. Glyn Dŵr could get no justice from king or parliament. This proud man, over forty and grey-haired in the royal service, was visited with insult and malice. Like a true marcher, he decided to avenge his honour with his sword.

But he was more than a marcher. He was the greatest living representative of the royal houses of Wales, an heir to Cadwaladr the Blessed. And if he ever forgot, the bards would remind him. Perhaps others would remind him too. Possibly, later history leads us to spy Tudors lurking behind every bush in north Wales at this time, but certainly, Rhys and Gwilym Tudor were with Owain from the beginning, and whether he acted entirely of his own volition, we shall never know. Joan of Arc, we know, heard voices from Heaven ; Owain Glyn Dŵr may have heard voices from Anglesey.

It was in September 1400 that a group of his supporters, with what an English jury called their wizard, proclaimed him prince of Wales. Parliament at once rushed anti-Welsh legislation on to the statute-book, as Welsh students and labourers in England flocked home to join the revolt, for the proclamation, however dubious its provenance and meaning, evoked an immediate response. And in the following year, Owain turned south, won a crushing victory near Plynlimon. Revolt ran like

wildfire through west Wales and an imperious letter went out
to his supporters in the south. This letter resolves the last
doubt. For in it Owain proclaims himself the liberator
appointed by God to deliver the Welsh race from its oppressors.

The war which followed was, for the English, largely a matter
of logistics, of relieving their isolated castles. Henry IV, beset
by Welsh, Scots, French and rebellious barons, never really got
to grips with it, and the revolt wore itself out, in a small country
exhausted beyond the limit of endurance. For the Welsh, it
was a peasant uprising which grew into a national war, their
leader flitting so swiftly and mysteriously from one storm-
centre to the next that in English eyes he grew to be an ogre
credited with occult powers, a name to frighten children with.
And there is something miraculous about his success.   For
within two years, outside south Pembroke and a few beleaguered
castles, Wales had been swept clear.

Inevitably the revolt was enmeshed in the web of English
baronial politics. The key here was the capture of Edmund
Mortimer in 1402, for by a curious quirk of circumstance the
Mortimers had the best legitimate claim both to the inheritance
of Llywelyn the Last and to the throne of England itself.
Henry IV, perhaps naturally, proved reluctant to ransom
Edmund. Glyn Dŵr embraced his cause, and sealed the
alliance with the marriage of Edmund to his daughter
Catherine. This opened a path for the Welshman into the
ranks of the dissident English baronage, produced a whole
crop of conspiracies — Henry Percy's rising of 1403, defeated
at Shrewsbury ; the Tripartite Indenture of 1405, where
Mortimer and the Percy earl of Northumberland proposed to
divide England between them, leaving to Glyn Dŵr a Wales
which was to run from Severn to Mersey, embracing great
tracts of western England, with a frontier deliberately drawn to
include the Six Ashes on the Bridgenorth road, where Merlin
had prophesied the Great Eagle would rally his Welsh warriors
for the day of deliverance. This attempt to transmute myth
into history failed, as did all others, through bad planning and
faulty co-ordination.

Owain had more luck with his foreign friends. As early as
1401, he had appealed to the Irish (in Latin) and to the Scots

(in French). Success awaited on the establishment of his own power. By 1404, this had been achieved. In that year, the great castles at Aberystwyth and Harlech fell, giving him a base, a court, a working capital. In the same period the revolt began to lose its nakedly social character, as the prudent, the circumspect, the men with something to lose, rallied belatedly to his cause. The intelligentsia came over — John Trevor, bishop of St. Asaph, Lewis Byford, bishop of Bangor, above all, Dr. Gruffydd Young, a trained lawyer who became Owain's chancellor and who was, without doubt, the author of his more ambitious projects. The adherence of these men, with their skill, their training, their European contacts, gave the movement coherence and backbone. Its tone becomes stridently self-confident.

These were the years of the famous parliaments at Machynlleth and Harlech ; of Owain's coronation before the envoys of France, Scotland and Castile ; the years of the French alliance. He is now Owain by the grace of God prince of Wales, with a great seal and a privy seal. He has taken over the coat of arms of Gwynedd, linking his cause to that of the state-builders, the two Llywelyns of the thirteenth century. Gruffydd Young and John Hanmer, his envoys to the court of France, were the envoys of an authentic prince.

And, in response to French demands for a transfer of church allegiance to the French anti-pope at Avignon, Owain evolved a constructive national policy which constitutes his chief claim to the title of statesman — the policy ratified by a synod of Welsh clerics at Pennal in 1406. The Welsh Church is to be free from Canterbury, with St. David's as its metropolitan ; Welsh clerics are to be Welsh-speaking, Welsh church revenues devoted to the needs of Wales. Finally, in a clause which has caught the imagination of posterity, two universities are to to be set up, one in the north, one in the south, to train Welshmen to the service of Wales.

This programme, in essence political, would have grounded the new principality on a firm base, had it ever gone into effect. But by 1406 the tide had already turned. At the French court, it was Louis of Orleans who won the day, and the main French effort went into Aquitaine. A missed opportunity, for a strong

French left hook through Wales would surely have unseated Henry IV. A small French force did land, at Milford Haven in 1405. It marched with the Welsh to Worcester, but then withdrew before Henry's army.

It was now that exhaustion began to tell. In 1406, outlying sectors of Wales fell away ; besieged castles became bases for reconquest. In 1408 came disaster. Harlech and Aberystwyth fell, Mortimer died, many of Glyn Dŵr's own family were taken prisoner. By 1410, Owain himself was once more a hunted outlaw. The last direct reference to him comes in 1412. After that, there is silence. Henry V, who had taken Owain's son into his service, offered the rebel a pardon twice. But the old man was apparently too proud to accept. No-one knows when he died or where he died. The happiest hypothesis places him in the Golden Valley among the Scudamores, but no-one knows. No bard sang his *marwnad*, his elegy. They knew he could not die ; one day he would return. With his disappearance Owain ceases to be a man. He becomes a legend.

His revolt acted as a catalyst. All the social processes at work before it were now enormously accelerated. Manorialism and the kindred crumbled rapidly ; Wales of the squires swiftly took shape in north and south, leaving the laggard central uplands to plague future governments with their legacy of disorder and banditry. The new gentry, cohering around the county courts, assumed increasingly the physiognomy and outlook of their counterparts across Offa's Dyke, so that in many parts of Wales, the Act of Union, when it came, merely gave legal definition to a social reality of long standing. The sheer destructiveness of the revolt, possibly overstated, if fifteenth-century church-building be any index of social wealth, nevertheless led to a financial breakdown. The accounts of the Principality become one long series of bankruptcy statements. In the end, union seemed the only answer to the fiscal problem. The revolt, in short, cleared the way for the new society. On the other hand, the immediate legacy was harsh. Welsh writing in the fifteenth century is bitterly anti-English. The old craving for a saviour remains, shot through now with bizarre prophecies of a Welsh conquest of the English throne, with a fevered and frequently artificial bardic quest for the returned Owain among the protagonists of the Wars of the Roses, so many of them descendants of men who had taken the winning side during the rising itself. And if there is doubt about Welsh national consciousness, even Welsh nationalism, before the revolt, there can be none after it, for the Welsh mind is still haunted by its lightning-flash vision of a people that was free.

That dualism, that dichotomy, that whole complex of conflicting, sometimes unpleasant emotions, which afflicts the conscious Welshman was, I believe, introduced into Welsh life, at least in its modern form, by the revolt. It is the rising, or rather that whole process of which the rising was at once cause and symptom, which has made us the peculiarly schizophrenic people we are.

Modern Wales, in short, really begins in 1410.

WALES IN FIFTEENTH-CENTURY POLITICS

By Evan D. Jones

SIR John Wynn of Gwydir's picture of the strife, feuds, and desolation of Owain Glyn Dŵr's rebellion has been accepted by modern historians. They have been impressed by the grass which grew in the market-place and the deer which fed in the churchyard at Llanrwst. Accounts of officers of the crown and of manors have been unrolled and they excuse decay of rents for decades on the score of the ruin left by the rebellion. Then, there are the repressive measures of 1401 and 1402 to remind us that the rebellion and its repression left dregs of bitterness. The Lancastrian penal code provoked a violent reaction against everything English for the remainder of the century — against English ways, English laws, English entertainment, English wives, English doctors, and above all English burgesses. ' Sais' and ' burgess ' became synonyms of evil connotation. When council and parliament tended to forget the penal code the burgesses by petition and complaint were ready to see that they did not become obsolete. A strict enforcement of the laws would deprive Welshmen of the most elementary rights of citizenship. No Welshman could acquire property in or near a borough, nor hold office under the crown, nor serve on juries, nor secure the conviction of an Englishman on his own oath. Inter-marriage between the two peoples was forbidden on pain of involving the English partner and the offspring in all the disabilities of Welshmen of full blood. The code was a most effective nurse of nationalism. But, except at times of crisis as in 1430 and 1447, the laws were virtually allowed to lapse after the death of Henry IV. When Henry V embarked on his French campaigns he welcomed Welsh captains and their bowmen, and they flocked to his service. David Gam, Roger Vaughan, Mathew Goch, Sir Richard Gethin, Sir Griffith Vaughan, Sir William ap Thomas, Sir William Herbert and

Owen Tudor wrote their names in the chronicles of England and France. Their exploits are recorded with pride in Welsh ode and ' cywydd.' Others found opportunities for service and self-advancement in civil administration at home. If Welshmen could not hold office under the crown, the English magnates, who held them nominally, had to rely upon Welsh deputies to carry out their duties in Welsh Wales. Humphrey, duke of Gloucester, trusted Griffith ap Nicholas even to hold sessions for him in Carmarthen and Cardigan. Whether as soldiers or as administrators the rising Welsh squirearchy was protected in high places and many Welshmen took the further precaution of enfranchisement by parliament to the great annoyance of burgesses in Wales and the disgust of Welsh poets who could not understand why anyone should want to buy English citizenship. The descendants of these ambitious Welshmen later on found their way into the ranks of the English peerage. But if the strong found security against the penal laws lesser men were often exposed to their rigours especially in the boroughs, as Lewis Glyn Cothi found to his great indignation when he settled in the Lancastrian stronghold of Chester. He retaliated with a poem begging a patron in Oswestry to give him a sword which he would whet upon the churls of Chester.

However bitter the dregs of the rebellion may have been, not one of the poets finds fault with Owain Glyn Dŵr. His real achievement of Welsh unity, even though of short duration, became in their minds a pattern for others in authority to follow. Welsh national consciousness was his creation. It gathered strength from repression. It was nurtured by the achievements of Welshmen at home and abroad, and it was strengthened by the dependence of both parties in the civil war upon Welsh support. This awakening of a national consciousness produced a remarkable corpus of poetry. The poets in their eulogies of prospective leaders always saw with the inward eye the shape of Owain Glyn Dŵr. His star shines brightly in many a ' cywydd', the dash of a gallant squire was simply his pomp revived, his blood was the country's surest protection, the outlaws in the hills were his men, the braves of many battles were his wolves and lions, Powys was his country, and Oswestry its London. As time rolled on the endearing epithet ' hen ' (old) became attached to his name, and he was the deliverer who would one day return.

The middle years of the century saw the Hundred Years' War draw to its sorry close. The troops came home in time for the civil strife which we call the Wars of the Roses, and with them the vineyards of France brought fresh flavours into Welsh verse. There is a richness reflected in the contemporary poetry which sharply contradicts much of the evidence of Tudor writers looking back over their shoulders towards the fifteenth century. This wealth was not confined to the flourishing houses but was also a feature of life in houses of more modest pretensions in the backwoods of Welsh Wales. However modest in appearance some of these houses must have been, their owners took pride in their blood and tradition and the poetry reflects an aristocratic culture. It is certainly not the product of deep depression.

At no time in its history did Wales play a more decisive part in English politics than in the quarter of a century between 1460 and 1485, and the poets were fully conscious of it. Whatever happened in England they were sure that a proper appeal to Wales would find response.

You will recall the general background. Richard, Duke of York, with the active support of the earl of Warwick, usually styled ' kingmaker,' had pressed his claim to the crown of England by an appeal to arms. The resources of the monarchy were hopelessly inadequate in the face of such a combination of territorial magnates. The king, Henry VI, was personally weak and he wore a crown usurped by his grandfather, Henry of Lancaster, in 1399. The forces under the duke of York's personal command were heavily defeated by the Lancastrians at Wakefield in December 1460, and he himself slain ; the Yorkist forces under the earl of Warwick suffered a similar fate at St. Alban's in February, 1461, but the fortunes of the House of York had been secured a fortnight earlier at Mortimer's Cross by Edward, the young earl of March, and his Welsh and Mortimer levies. Edward made his way to London where he was crowned as Edward IV. The earl of Warwick who had escaped with his life at St. Albans continued to support

Edward until a final break in 1470 when he changed his allegiance. Henry VI was restored for a few months, but in April 1471 Edward returned from exile and defeated the earl of Warwick at Barnet and the remainder of the Lancastrian forces at Tewkesbury. Henry VI obligingly died ' of pure displeasure and melancholy', and Edward IV resumed his reign with the position of the monarchy greatly strengthened by the confiscation of a large proportion of the estates of the powerful earl of Warwick and of the Lancastrian leaders. He was therefore able to hold his crown unchallenged till his death in 1483. It was the personal character of the usurper, Richard III, more than the weakness of the crown that made it possible for Henry Tudor to supplant the House of York in 1485.

In 1460, Wales was almost equally divided between the two parties of York and Lancaster. The latter drew its support almost entirely from the western side of the country where the two divisions of the Principality lay. The duchy of Lancaster also controlled considerable areas in south Wales. The earldom of Pembroke was then in the hands of Jasper Tudor, half-brother and loyal supporter of Henry VI. The eastern half of Wales, where the Mortimer interest was strong, was predominantly Yorkist in sympathy. The earl of Warwick in Glamorgan, and the Nevilles in Gwent, were of the same party. Indeed, apart from the county of Flint, the only considerable Lancastrian power in east Wales was the Stafford lordship of Brecknock. The shifting of the balance of power from marcher lords to the crown within a short space of time was as striking in Wales as it was in England and did more than anything else to shatter Owain Glyn Dŵr's dream of a Wales independent of the English crown. With Edward IV's triumph in 1461, the power of the two sections of the Principality, the Lancastrian lordships, and the Mortimer inheritance, were consolidated behind the crown. The only weakness was the hold which Jasper Tudor was able to maintain through Harlech until 1468. With the death of the earl of Warwick in 1471, the lordship of Glamorgan also fell into the hands of the crown, and to strengthen his hold on Wales still further, Edward persuaded the second earl of Pembroke in 1479 to take the earldom of Huntingdon in exchange for Pembroke. The duke o

Buckingham's attainder in 1483 brought about the forfeiture of the lordship of Brecknock and to all intents and purposes completed the process of liquidating the great marcher lordships.

The more or less equal division of power between the two contending parties in Wales at the beginning of the Wars of the Roses is clearly reflected in Welsh poetry. The territorial distribution of patronage had to affect the poets' politics. A Welsh bard by the canons of his craft was bound to extol his patron's loyalty to his overlord wherever his own personal sympathies might lie. Lewis Glyn Cothi was at first a staunch Lancastrian along with his patrons, Griffith ap Nicholas and his sons, but he also sang much to the descendants of Sir Dafydd Gam, who were firm Yorkists. He lived long enough to return in 1483 to his first allegiance. Other poets also present a similar stratification in their work, corresponding to the varying fortunes of the great protagonists. By his residence in the principality Tudur Penllyn shared the Lancastrian sympathies of the house of Corsygedol and was a great admirer of the defenders of Harlech Castle. Guto'r Glyn and Huw Cae Llwyd, on the other hand, had their patrons mainly on Mortimer ground, and they were decidedly Yorkist in sympathy. Still, the bards could visit houses of rival parties, generally without fear. There may have been cases of extreme aggravation as in the case of the execution of Sir Roger Vaughan at Chepstow by Jasper Tudor's command in 1471. A poet closely identified with Jasper's cause would keep away from Tretower for some time after that. But normally there was easy coming and going and the poems reflect the different allegiances of the patrons. Lewis Glyn Cothi in the days of his first ardour for Jasper Tudor describes how he was teased about him in a Yorkist house in Radnorshire, but the welcome was no less cordial.

Those of you who know the Wars of the Roses only from your school history books would find the Welsh view of the struggle rather different. The relative importance of battles and personalities are not the same in Welsh poetry as they are in English history books. The Welsh poets were touched more by Mortimer's Cross, 1461, the defence of Harlech Castle from

1461, and its fall in 1468, the battle of Banbury, 1469, and Bosworth.   Of these, Bosworth is probably the only name that remains to you from your history books.   The actors in the drama are as different as the incidents.   In Welsh poetry, apart from the kings, Henry VI, Edward IV, and Richard III, the outstanding personalities are William Herbert, earl of Pembroke, Jasper Tudor, ' brother and uncle of kings', and Sir Rhys ap Thomas.

William Herbert's rise to prominence, indeed to eminence, was meteoric and his spell of glory was brief.   Set upon the background of Welsh civil disabilities his achievements dazzled the poets.   At Edward's side when the sun burst double at Mortimer's Cross he became his right hand man when he assumed the crown a few weeks later.   In the same year, 1461, Herbert became Chief Justice and Chamberlain of South Wales, and a peer as Lord Herbert. Next year he became a Knight of the Garter.   Honours, offices, and lordships were showered upon him.   In 1466, he saw his son and heir married to the queen's sister.   In 1467 he was made Chief Justice of North Wales and in 1468 led the expedition into Gwynedd which robbed Jasper Tudor of his last stronghold, Harlech castle.   The stubborn defence by the tiny garrison had won the admiration of the poets and Dafydd Llwyd rejoiced that little Harlech alone had remained true to the feeble crown.   When Harlech fell Guto'r Glyn appealed to Lord Herbert to further the cause of Wales.   He pleaded for leniency towards the Welsh and a reversal of the operation of the penal laws.   Herbert should not attempt to levy a tax which could not be collected and he should spare the lives of Welsh Lancastrian leaders who were patrons of the bards. The children of Rowenna should not be allowed to remain in Gwynedd nor the children of Horsa in Flint.   No Englishman should retain office in Wales and there should be no pardon for a single burgess.   He should draw all Welshmen together, uniting them from Glamorgan to Gwynedd, from Conway to Neath.   Should he by this offend England and her dukes Wales would stand by him.   This was typical of the spirit of self-confidence inspired by Owain Glyn Dŵr and now revived by William Herbert's success.

In fact the English nobility represented by the earl of Warwick were offended because Edward IV had at his side upstarts like Lord Herbert, and the northern Lancastrians rose in rebellion at Warwick's instigation in 1469. Herbert, created earl of Pembroke after his capture of Harlech, was summoned to take his forces via Gloucester towards London. Before setting out he arranged an eve of campaign feast at Raglan. Guto'r Glyn wrote a poem on the occasion full of foreboding. He feared for his patron for he knew how jealous of him the children of Rowenna had become. It was as poison to them to have a Welsh-speaking earl. Herbert was Roland if Edward was Charlemagne, a comparison used a few years earlier by Lewis Glyn Cothi. When Edward went to war Herbert was his limb, his elbow, his hand, and his foot. He was called to the council on everything. He was the keeper of Edward's peace.

Guto'r Glyn's forebodings were justified. The battle of Banbury was lost in the last week of July, 1469, the flower of the Welsh march fell on the field, and the earl of Pembroke and his brother, Sir Richard Herbert, were executed by Warwick's command. Banbury produced a large number of elegies and its memory burned for years in the hearts of Welshmen. The very name was identified with treachery and the death of Warwick at the battle of Barnet two years afterwards was hailed by the poets as retribution for Banbury.

The earl of Pembroke's record in Welsh poetry is unsullied, for his Welshness was never in doubt and he did not live long enough to produce the disillusionment which would have inevitably followed a longer tenure of high office under the crown. In the fifteenth century Welshness was the key to bardic favour. Edward IV by virtue of descent from Gwladys Ddu was accepted as a Welshman, an early example of that fatal trait of credulity in the Welsh mind. The blood of Llywelyn Fawr was pretty thin in Mortimer veins before it came to Edward IV. Dafydd Llwyd ap Llewelyn ap Griffith argued at one time that as a Welshman Edward IV was to be preferred to Jasper Tudor whom so many looked upon as a son of prophecy. However, when Edward fled to his native Rouen it was to Jasper that Dafydd Llwyd turned. When suspicion fell on Henry Tudor's Welshness some years later Dafydd

Llwyd warned him to beware if he was an Englishman. In that burst of prophetic frenzy after 1483 Dafydd Llwyd was as eloquent as any of the disciples of Geoffrey of Monmouth in conjuring the illusion that Welsh nationalism would be crowned in London. Vaticination had been an element in the works of the classic poets, now it ran wild.

Ellis Griffith, the soldier-chronicler of Calais, relates a legend about a taunt by the abbot of Valle Crucis that Owain Glyn Dŵr had risen too early by a hundred years. This was a sixteenth-century fabrication. It could not have appeared before 1485. Had Owain not risen when he did the fifteenth century in Welsh poetry would have been very different, and there would have been no Welsh nation to survive into modern times.

THE RISE OF THE HOUSE OF TUDOR

By David Williams

THE year 1485 is the conventionally accepted date for the ending of the Middle Ages in England and Wales. In point of fact it marks only the end of the Wars of the Roses, for Bosworth proved to be the last battle in that disastrous struggle. And, even so, we know this to be true only through the hindsight which history gives us ; contemporaries cannot possibly have been certain that the war would not break out again ; they were not conscious of so distinct a break. The division of history into periods is, at best, a matter of convenience. Social conditions and trends of development, even forms of government, often continue unaffected by spectacular events. Of this particular break the late A. F. Pollard, who was possibly the greatest of all sixteenth century specialists, said that ' the careful student of Henry VII's reign is less concerned with things which began under Henry VII than with things which did not end with Richard III'. It may well be that the year 1536, the date of the Act of Union, provides a better dividing line as far as Wales is concerned. Yet it would be pedantic to reject a convention which is now so long-established. Besides, the accession to the throne of England of Henry Tudor in 1485 is, after all, an event of the utmost significance in the history of Wales. How it came about, and what its significance was, are the topics which I now hope to discuss.

To do so it is necessary, in the first place, to account for the rise of the house of Tudor, and in this I rely upon a very remarkable piece of research by Professor Glyn Roberts published by him under the title of ' Wyrion Eden ' in the *Anglesey Antiquarian Society Transactions* for 1951. The founder of the Tudor family was Ednyfed Fychan, seneschal to the princes of Gwynedd, that is, Llywelyn the Great and his son David, from about 1215 till his death in 1246. His sons served in the same capacity under Llywelyn ap Gruffydd, the last independent prince of Wales. Ironically enough, the fall of the house of Gwynedd did not bring ruin to this particular family. Some of its members undoubtedly became supporters of the English crown, an example of how dangerous it is to import twentieth-century ideas of patriotism into the Middle Ages. It was in the century which succeeded the death of Llywelyn ap Gruffydd that the family experienced the greatest prosperity, and this was typical of the class of gentry and officials which was then emerging in Wales. The seneschal's great-great-grandson, Tudur ap Goronwy, held extensive lands in the mid-fourteenth century. Of these possessions, Penmynydd in Anglesey passed to his eldest son Goronwy. This is the so-called ' home of the Tudors', but its connection with the Tudor dynasty was slight — merely that it belonged to the descendants of Henry VII's great-grandfather's eldest brother. Strange to say, the squires of Penmynydd do not seem to have taken advantage of the accession of Henry VII to the throne. They remained content with the part they played in local affairs, until the total eclipse of the family towards the end of the seventeenth century.

The revolt of Owain Glyn Dŵr, in the first decade of the fifteenth century, was far more disastrous to the family than the Edwardian conquest had been. Through their mother, the sons of Tudur ap Goronwy were first cousins of Glyn Dŵr, and they threw in their lot with him. In consequence their lands were forfeited, though Penmynydd was eventually re-stored to them. One of the brothers, Rhys, was executed at Chester in 1412. It is the role of another brother, Maredudd, which is obscure. He is said to have been steward to the bishop of Bangor. According to tradition he had fled from Wales because of some crime he had committed. Yet his son, Owain (who bore the name of the rebel chieftain), became a page in the household of King Henry V, another instance of the difficulty one encounters if one thinks of loyalty in the Middle Ages in terms of the twentieth century. This page, Owain ap Maredudd ap Tudur, took a surname, English fashion. He chose his grand-father's name and became Owen Tudor. It is intriguing to think that had he taken his father's name, Maredudd, England would have had not a Tudor but a Meredith dynasty.

Owen Tudor's career is familiar to most people. His master, the king, died in 1422, two years after his marriage with Catherine of Valois, who thus became a widow before she had reached the age of twenty-one. She fell in love with Owen Tudor, who was handsome, and graceful, and about her own age. The late judge, Sir Thomas Artemus Jones, devoted an article in the *Bulletin of the Board of Celtic Studies* for 1943 to the problem of whether they were ever married. At best the judge's verdict is inconclusive. They certainly had four children, three sons and a daughter, of whom Edmund and Jasper alone concern us. According to the sixteenth-century historian, Sir John Wynn of Gwydir, Catherine was visited by her Welsh in-laws, but they spoke no English, and she thought them ' the goodliest dumb creatures that she ever saw'. After Catherine's death Owen Tudor got into difficulties, but the boy King, Henry VI, took his step-father into favour, made his half-brother, Edmund, earl of Richmond, and his half-brother, Jasper, earl of Pembroke. He also arranged the marriage of Edmund with Margaret Beaufort, daughter of the duke of Somerset, the momentous marriage which later gave Edmund's son, Henry Tudor, his claim to the throne. Owen Tudor naturally supported his step-son, the king, when civil war — the Wars of the Roses — broke out, but he was taken prisoner early in the war and was executed at Hereford. He is said to have remarked ruefully as he laid his head on the block that it was ' wont to lie in queen Catherine's lap'.

Edmund Tudor was already dead. What connection he had with Wales is not known, but it was at Carmarthen that he died on 3 November 1456, and he was buried in the Grey Friars there. When that house was dissolved in 1536, his remains were removed to the choir of St. David's Cathedral, and his tomb is now the outstanding monument at St. David's. His child was born posthumously, in his brother, Jasper's, great castle at Pembroke, on 28 January, 1457. It is strange to think that the mother, Lady Margaret Beaufort, had not then yet reached the age of fourteen. She was to become one of the most remarkable women in England in the Middle Ages, a patron of religion and of learning and founder of St. John's College, Cambridge. The child, Henry Tudor, was cared for by his uncle, Jasper, who sponsored his cause in the Wars of the Roses. The disastrous defeat of the Lancastrians at the battle of Tewkesbury in 1471 seemed to bring that war to an end, but it also made Henry Tudor the Lancastrian claimant to the throne through his mother, Lady Margaret. It was now of supreme importance that the boy should not fall into Yorkist hands, and Jasper took him abroad. They sailed from Tenby ; strong winds compelled them to land in Brittany. The boy was then fourteen years of age ; for the next fourteen years he remained in exile.

The exiled prince caught the imagination of the Welsh people who rallied to his support, and the bards kept them in a ferment of expectation. They spoke of him as Arthur, who would rescue the Welsh from thraldom, and as Glyn Dŵr whose mysterious disappearance led some to believe that he would again return. Of all these vaticinatory bards none was more prolific than Dafydd Llwyd ap Llywelyn of Mathafarn, near Machynlleth, whom I shall mention later.

The death of Edward IV, and the usurpation of the throne by the odious tyrant, Richard III, revived the hopes of the exiles. Richard III entrusted the government of Wales to Henry Stafford, second duke of Buckingham, the greatest of all the marcher lords, who had inherited the vast lands of the lord-ship of Brecon. Nevertheless Buckingham deserted to Henry Tudor. A general rising was planned for October 1483, but it ended in disaster, for gales dispersed Henry's fleet, and great floods in the Severn prevented Buckingham's advance, so that he was captured and executed. The exiles returned to Rennes, and there, on Christmas Day, in the great cathedral, with the snow lying thick outside, they all bound themselves to each other and to their prince, and he promised to marry Elizabeth of York thereby uniting the White Rose with the Red. But a new complication arose when they found that the Breton government might betray them, and they hurriedly left for France. There they continued their preparations, and, at long last, on the 1st of August 1485, Jasper and Henry sailed from the mouth of the Seine with a force of two thousand men.

They landed at Dale, a secluded bay just within Milford Haven (on the north side) a little before sunset on Sunday evening, the 7th of August. The great magnate of south-west Wales was Rhys ap Thomas of Dinefwr, who, through his mother, had in his veins the blood of the ancient princes of Deheubarth. A seventeenth century life of Sir Rhys, which naturally sought to magnify his part in this glorious expedition, dramatically describes his arrival at Dale, mounted on his famous horse, Llwyd y Bacse, and surrounded by his forces, to welcome the prince. Rhys, according to this account, had given his oath to king Richard that Harry of Richmond would advance only over his body, so he dutifully lay down on the ground for the prince to step over him. Another tradition says that he got under Mullock Bridge when the prince passed over. Unfortunately there is no evidence that he was there at all ; on the contrary it is most unlikely that he was. At daybreak on Monday, Henry, with his motley assortment of Frenchmen, Bretons and Welsh soldiers, and their baggage and camp followers, moved on to Haverfordwest, which they reached before noon. Then they crossed the Presely hills into the parish of Nevern, where the prince is supposed to have stayed at Ragwr-lwyd. This would mean a considerable march of thirty miles in one day, much of it over difficult mountain tracks. On Tuesday they proceeded through Cardigan, where the prince halted, presumably for refreshment, at the Three Mariners, and then on, following the coast, for another dozen miles or so to Llwyn Dafydd in the parish of Llandisilio-gogo. Here he was the guest of Dafydd ab Ifan, to whom Henry VII later on presented the ' hirlas ' or drinking horn now in the possession of the earl of Cawdor. The prince is then supposed to have stayed, again, seven miles further on, at Wern Dafydd in the parish of Llanarth, the guest of Einon ap Dafydd Llwyd, but it is highly improbable that he spent two nights in this neighbourhood. He continued to follow the coast, and on Thursday crossed the Dyfi near Machynlleth. He is reputed to have proceeded to Mathafarn, to consult the prophet and poet, Dafydd Llwyd ap Llywelyn. Prophecy in general terms had been easy, but foretelling the outcome of a specific event was not so easy, and the poet in his predicament consulted his wife, who told him to prophesy victory, for if the prince were successful he might offer him a reward, but if he were not successful they were unlikely ever to hear from him. What and rural deans were to be the key men. They were usually of Welsh origin and in close touch with priests and people. But theirs was no easy task. Progress was slow, and compromises and failures were inevitable. There was one notoriously difficult problem on which the disciplinary machine always tended to break its teeth. That was the celibacy of the clergy. The Church found it impossible to enforce this generally, and right down to the eve of the Reformation most Welsh parish priests took wives.

The ideal of celibacy found more willing adherents among the religious orders. I have spoken of the failure of the Benedictines to make any impression on the Welsh. But the Cistercians or White Monks were conspicuously successful. This was chiefly because they were not associated in Welsh minds with alien conquest. Far from being timid henchmen of the Normans who clung to the skirts of castle and borough, the Cistercians sought out the solitude of mountain and moorland. Their austere discipline seemed to reincarnate the ideals of the Celtic saints. Their emphasis on pastoral farming fitted well into the stock-rearing economy of Wales, though not as smoothly and unresentedly as is sometimes suggested. The Cistercians won a unique place in the affections of princes and people. Their houses became havens of ordered worship, cradles of learning, patrons of literature, and pioneers in the arts of flock-management and wool production. Names like Strata Florida, Conway, Valle Crucis, Margam and Tintern are among the most hallowed in the history of religion in medieval Wales.

By the thirteenth century the initiative among religious orders was tending to pass to the new orders of friars. The friars moved freely among the people, the Franciscans in their grey habit, and the Dominicans in black. Both orders were very well received in Wales. From their midst were drawn some of the foremost scholars and bishops of medieval Wales. Such a one was Anian, bishop of St. Asaph from 1268 to 1293. This fiery Dominican came from a line of princes and warriors. Thin-skinned, hot-blooded, and obstinate, a tremendous stickler for the rights of his see, he was willing to press his claims against Welsh abbots or English bishops, king only along the Normanized fringes and built in the shadow of Norman castles, they were almost as much an instrument of conquest as the castle or borough. Not one Benedictine house flourished in those parts of Wales held for any length of time by the Welsh princes. To the end of their existence the Black Monks in Wales were recruited from a non-Welsh population.

But we should be getting an entirely false perspective of the medieval Church if we thought of it only as an instrument of political subjection. The impact of the Norman Conquest also had immense consequences for good. The isolation of the pre-Norman church in Wales carried with it the peril of stagnation as the price of autonomy. By breaking down this isolation the Normans threw the Church open to fresh and invigorating streams of reform flowing strongly from the Continent. One of the most decisive consequences was to bring the Welsh Church into more intimate relationship with the fountainhead of medieval religion, the reformed papacy. To Rome the most active and zealous Welsh clerics looked for inspiration and guidance. From Rome came much of the driving force behind the transforming of the organization and government of the Church in Wales.

This transformation is indeed the most enduring achievement of the medieval Church. One of the first tasks was to change the mother-daughter relationship of Celtic bishoprics into territorially-defined dioceses. That is, instead of a bishop having authority over a number of widely-scattered churches which regarded his church as their mother-church, he now ruled over a fixed geographical area. Within these territorial dioceses, other new ecclesiastical boundaries were being mapped out. Archdeaconries and rural deaneries came into being for the first time. The rural deanery was usually based on the civil unit of the commote or the cantref, and the archdeaconry on a province. Parishes, too, were being carved out on a territorial basis for the first time — a slow and difficult job which was not completed in north Wales until well on into the fourteenth century.

One of the main purposes of the new territorial organization of the Church was to pave the way for the introduction of stricter canons of discipline. In this process the archdeacons profession of obedience to the see of Canterbury. This set the pattern for the future. By the middle of the twelfth century bishops of all four Welsh dioceses had been induced to make this profession. The first and decisive stage of bringing the Welsh Church under the control of king and archbishop had been accomplished. It was a change big with consequences for Church and people, comparable in scope and magnitude with those later to be brought about by the Protestant Reformation and the Methodist Revival.

This new relationship between the Welsh bishops and Canterbury was not readily accepted in Wales. The princes of Gwynedd, following the line set by Owain Gwynedd in the twelfth century, regarded the diocese of Bangor as their own special preserve and were unwilling to allow the influence of Canterbury to be extended over the see. In south Wales Gerald the Welshman, himself three parts a Norman, was to become the most vigorous champion of the right of the Welsh Church to independence of Canterbury. For a quarter of a century from 1176 onwards he fought a campaign to have St. David's recognized as the seat of an archbishopric independent of Canterbury. Quarrelsome, witty, voluble, opinionated, eloquent, conceited and indefatigable, Gerald pleaded his case in season and out of season, in St. David's and at the papal curia, among clergy and laity. Flattering, castigating, persuading and exhorting, he employed all the resources of one of the liveliest tongues and swiftest pens known to the Middle Ages. And all, alas, in vain !

Another major step taken by the Normans to destroy the Celtic organization of the Church was to break up the *clas* wherever possible. The *clas* consisted of a body of canons, usually hereditary, attached to a mother church. Wherever the Normans were strongly established, *clasau* were suppressed and their endowments transferred to monasteries in England or on the Continent. In this way the venerable *clas* founded by Illtud at Llantwit Major perished and its possessions passed to the abbey of Tewkesbury.

Closely connected with this step of breaking up the *clasau* was the introduction of Latin type monasteries into Wales. The first to be founded were those of the Benedictine order. Found

church to have his union with a wife solemnized by the sacrament of marriage. As he approached the threshold of death he
received forgiveness of mortal sins when extreme unction was
administered to him. Just as his body had to have food so his
soul needed the sustenance of mass ; and just as his bodily
ailments needed healing so the disorders of his soul must be
cleansed by the sacrament of penance.

For all the passing seasons of the year the Church had its
Christian calendar. At all the great festivals there were
appropriate services and ceremonies. At Christmas, churches
and houses were brightened by silent representations of the
scene at Bethlehem. Ashes were received on Ash Wednesday
as a token of the defilement of sin. On Palm Sunday the
congregation bore palms and sang " Hosanna" to welcome a
procession of priests. On Good Friday and Easter Sunday they
re-enacted the burial and resurrection of Jesus. There was no
point in human life to which the influence of the Church did
not penetrate. Public health, charity, education, scholarship,
and the arts ; all fell beneath its sway. It very largely created
the medieval civilization, of which churches great and small
are the most characteristic memorials.

So great was the spiritual and intellectual authority of the
Church and so extensive its possessions that, in the eleventh
century, when the Normans came to Wales, they were bound to
try to exercise control over it. In Wales they found a Church
which was still markedly Celtic in character. Its discipline and
institutions differed widely from those with which the Normans
were familiar. This was a state of affairs which the intruders
would tolerate no longer than they had to. Pious, according to
their lights, as well as practical, they were able to reinforce
their political need to control the Church with an agreeable
sense of a religious mission to introduce reform. The individual
lords who carried out the conquest piecemeal were not the only
ones to realize the need for controlling the Church. The king
of England and his archbishop of Canterbury were no less
aware of its importance.

The first step, from which all else might follow, was to gain
control over the election of bishops. In 1107, Urban the first
Norman bishop of Llandaff, was induced to make the first